THE DARK STRETCH

A Young Wife's Miraculous Ride from Darkness to Light

RANDI E. STUMP

This book is written for my children: those here and those yet to come. May you know the story, the miracle. The importance of it all.

To Graham: You were perfectly chosen for this. Like Jacob with his limp, you have your own scar to walk with. May you never forget how far the Lord has brought you and how much He loves you. Loves us.

And to my most important:
The Greatest Horseman who ever lived,
My Lord, My Trainer, My closest Friend.

INTRODUCTION

By Christine Wyrtzen

A believer's love for God is often corrupted by tribulation, distress, persecution and danger. Distrust can spread like cancer. But though God's child pulls back from Him, He does not reciprocate. His love is ever present and engaging.

What happened to Randi and Graham will happen to all of us, in one way or another. There will be something cataclysmic that brings us to the end of ourselves. That's how it is on fallen earth. A phone call, a doctor's diagnosis, even a life-altering accident, will take us to the edges of our coping skills. What happens to faith at that point? How will we manage our inside world?

There is a roadmap for navigating pain and suffering. This story, related without the slightest pretense, will show us how it's done. Randi would cringe just hearing me say that for she doesn't see herself as a model of anything! But the Word of God was the rudder that kept her head on straight when her heart was on a roller coaster. Good theology was a necessity. While her emotions were tossed around like twigs in a tornado, God's promises held her beliefs in check.

See how a couple survives. See how parents and siblings cope with tragedy. See how an extended family supports one another.

But mostly, see how God became Randi's strong tower when the voice of the accuser came against her in a weakened condition. She clung, as a cherished daughter of her heavenly Father, to every Word He spoke while His arms held her fast. She learned first hand that 'neither death nor life, nor angels nor rulers, nor things present nor things to come, nor powers, nor height nor depth, nor anything else in all creation, could separate her from the love of God in Christ Jesus.' Romans 8:39

Her willingness to walk through the journey again, in story form, will serve forever to display the power and glory of God. Way to go, Randi!

PROLOGUE

July 2009

She's wild and unruly—her manners unmanageable. Her beauty is sleek and refined even for her young age. The most fit and able she has ever been, her power is untested, her strength unrealized. Muscles trace legs as strong as tree trunks. She could cause some serious damage.

Still, her eyes are kind. There's something special about her. Something unique. If only someone would take the time to develop her like digging out a precious jewel, discovering a priceless heirloom, hidden and then brought to glory. She was worth it.

Her strength, her intimidation, does not deter him. He uses it to his advantage. His jaw ticks, yet he's completely at ease. He has done this before. Rough hands show his marriage to hard work, yet his gentle fingers remain calm. He rolls his shirtsleeves up, one, two times. He's ready to get started.

The dust hangs heavy, the early morning dew a suspended pool waiting for the dip. They both breathe it in, different species completely, yet together in this circle, this ring made of hollow steel and metal. Round. About 60 feet across. And he holds her captive here against her will, against her resolve.

Sweat pours down his back; steam lifts off hers. It disappears into the dense fog. Air passes through two sets of burning lungs and meets the world as white breath. Thick. They're both tired. Every cell within her screams to run faster, to dodge his danger. But, she can't shake him who pursues her relentlessly.

She has spent her life in this race. It's in her blood, a battle her ancestors fought as they too faced this familiar enemy: Man.

It's quiet. Her hooves are the only sound as they beat out an even rhythm through the soft dirt underneath. Steady, constant, she moves away, farther and farther still, with no goal in mind but to escape him. Round and round and round again. This doesn't seem fair; she's trapped with nowhere to go.

Body pressing against the edges, she is caught between a freedom she knows is on the other side and a lifetime of slavery she feels is certain if she stays. There is no possible escape. She doesn't have an option, so she sticks to what she knows best. Running.

Chests heave and legs burn as the two struggle, together yet separated by something so powerful, so detrimental. A once perfect union between every man and creature is gone. For now. In its place is darkness. An unwelcome twist man brought on himself through his selfish ambition to be something better. Something he'll never be. It crept in and never left, staying to disrupt and destroy.

His crime. *His* offense. *His* sin separated them.

The only thing left for them now is the constant drip of sweat and struggle, muscles flexed in the contest for dominance. She craves relief but groans in agony. Her tail swishes in defiance. She blows and snorts in rebuke. It's one last effort. The end is near.

Her will for supremacy cannot match that of the man. From the beginning, man has ruled over her. He has dominion over her, over it all. She has no choice but to begin her surrender to him.

She sends out the signal—her white flag raised and carried through battle in the form of lowering her head, licking her lips. And to her surprise, he notices. He steps back watching carefully, his gaze traveling over her neck, shoulder, legs. But not in her eyes. Not yet.

He's waiting for a conversation to begin, a story to unfold. And it does. She turns her ear slightly toward him. It's not much, but it's a most significant start. This simple, quiet act speaks more to this man than any fancy speech from his own kind. She's finally ready, finally willing. Her curiosity won.

While the world sleeps, it's just starting for the man and this horse. The sun peeks its rays, anxious to see. The early morning songbirds respond with a tune of celebration. He pauses to listen. He smacks his lips and tastes the salt of his own skin. The sun stretches out completely now, piercing through the dust that drifts back home to the ground. The earth warms and shines.

The horse moves forward again, fast and sure, muscles trembling and quivering from work. She doesn't yet realize that the purpose for her life waits just feet away, not in slavery, but in more freedom than she can possibly imagine.

It's impossible for her to speak his words, his language, yet he's fluent in hers. His actions, his movements all say something to her. And she's listening.

He steps back again this time catching her attention and forcing her to make a decision. She hopes she makes the right one.

She stops and turns fast to face him. Her eyes search his. What does he want?

He steps forward, his hand outstretched in some kind of introduction. Her nostrils flare with each breath; her muzzle drips sweat. She can't bring herself to move.

He drops his eyes to the ground and takes another step. Another. And another. He moves in a zig-zag fashion, careful not to look into her eyes, for to lock in at this crucial moment would threaten her, strike fear in her. It would undo much of his work.

He's almost there. Almost to her. But instead of continuing on, he stops just feet away. This is the closest she allows him to come. Hand out, eyes dropped, it happens. The moment he's been waiting for. The one he knew would come.

Her nose extends tentatively. The thing she fears most stands close. And she can't help herself. She's curious. She can't reach him. She'll need to give more. Her body rocks slightly as she debates what to do. Her ears flick side to side. One hoof moves. Then another. Her breath blows hot, reaching the back of his hand and bouncing back to her face. His skin is soft, his smell unlike anything she's experienced before. It's not as scary as she thought it would be.

It's a horseman's handshake. A hello of sorts. The extension of his hand, the lengthening of her nose meeting for the first time; it's the most important beginning for them.

He looks her in the eyes for the first time. His voice is soft, comforting. She returns his gaze. She doesn't run in fear; this time she stays. His hand continues up her face rubbing carefully, wiping away all her doubts, her trepidations. It rests right between her eyes, the largest ones on land. They're so deep, where life and light and thoughts abound. For a moment he's lost in them, unable to break away. The bond is set, formed.

There is much to be done. Hours of training and repetition and wet saddle pads will have to wait. For today, this is enough. "It is good."

He turns to go, to release her back with the others. His boots cross to a gate latched with pegs. He hears the sound of her footsteps following right behind, going with him. She even touches him again; his lower back, his shoulder, sniffing and discovering. He can feel her breath. It's not so hot and fast now.

He glances toward the heavens, thin clouds easing across the sky. And he can't help but think of his life, once just like this horse behind him. Ragged, lost, unsure.

He's thankful for that introduction he received, the handshake that saved him. He smiles, remembering his Master reaching out, touching him softly, rubbing away his own doubts and frustrations. They were the gentlest of hands—trustworthy, experienced. Ones bearing deep scars with the skin a different color where the holes had been—holes this horseman helped put there.

1
A BLOOD BAY COLT

'It is not the critic who counts, not the man who points out how the strong man stumbled, or where the doer of deeds could have done better. The credit belongs to the man who is actually in the arena, whose face is marred by dust and sweat and blood, who strives valiantly, who errs and comes short again and again, who knows the great enthusiasms, the great devotions, and spends himself in a worthy cause, who at best knows achievement and who at the worst if he fails at least fails while daring greatly so that his place shall never be with those cold and timid souls who know neither victory nor defeat.'
~Theodore Roosevolt

One Year Later. July 30, 2010.

The tiny breeze collided with his warm chest—a welcoming feeling to hot lungs. He breathed it easily, calm. Small droplets of sweat appeared on his blood-colored coat above his flank, near his mouth with some even running off his fetlocks and disappearing into the churned soil below his hooves. His eyes glanced up at the clouds, thin and gliding easily through the summer sky with the same breeze that moved past him just moments before.

1

He knew dusk was near and with it the start of something only he and his partner shared. His commission in life to prove his obedience and bond came every week at the start of the rodeo. He understood every ounce of pressure above and beside him and was determined to succeed. Designed to follow, trained to trust, it had taken years of discipline and endless hours of hard work to get here. What he shared with this man was all he would ever know. It started in the circle of metal and steel like all the other horses.

He was warm and ready.

"Alright Crockett, what'd you say we get this show on the road?" Graham leaned forward in the saddle and patted the shiny shoulder. The horse was sleek and muscled. He quivered under Graham's tender touch. A hungry horsefly landed for a quick meal, but Graham smacked it and frowned, blood now smearing his palm. Without thought, he wiped the residue on his black chaps, erasing all evidence of the annoyance. He fingered the fringe that lined the length of his leg and checked his shirt, blue and buttoned straight, signifying his team. A number plastered his back while a cream-colored cowboy hat held firm, the inside sweatband doing its job well. The hat, much like the boots and bronze spurs, set the teams apart.

"I saw that," I said as I walked toward Graham. The horse I was waiting to ride followed close behind with his thick leather reins draped over my arm. He nuzzled me, suggesting it was time to go.

Graham smiled as I shoved the night's schedule into his hands.

"Don't lose that." I turned, my eyes taking in the gathering crowds near the fencing.

The folded paper slipped into his back pocket. At the same time, people slipped into bleachers, folding chairs or blankets. The excitement was evident. Children loped through dirt and grass with cap guns in hand shooting at whatever their imaginations could create—an Indian, a bandit. If one came to fight, there were plenty of little cowboys and sheriffs around to take control.

We left our own two boys with my mother for the night. They would have to grow into their boots a bit more before venturing to the ranch. The plights that awaited them were endless, and I smiled at the possibilities. Wyatt, a lean yet muscled 2-year-old carried his father's mysterious air, while young 11-month-old Keith wore just about everything on his sleeves, including his lunch and the pile of dirt he climbed earlier that day. How two boys could be so different is something I will never understand.

"It's time," I told Graham shifting my mind back to work.

We made our way to a cluster of thick pine surrounding wranglers and horses mixed with leather, sweat, and smells. The trees welcomed us into their fold, shielding us from so much more than just hot rays during the long dusty summer. In the middle, a dug out firepit smoked and spit its last breath of life, adding to our already filled nostrils. I wrinkled my nose and prepared for prayer. Worn hats left their homes, and words lifted to Heaven. I scanned the crew of wranglers—like family to me. Brows marked a type of dirt that couldn't be washed away, and calloused hands showcased an endless amount of hard work.

Nervous eyes lifted at the end, and boots scraped into stirrups. I ran through my safety checklist, clearly expecting something to be amiss. Horses saddled, flag holders secured, helmets ready for bulldogging, cows penned, wranglers lined and ready.

I was pleased to find all as it should be. We were in for a perfect night, a great rodeo.

I mounted up.

My clammy hand reached for a flag and forced it into its holder. The wooden pole rubbed my worn wranglers but soon nestled comfortably against my right boot. The bright material draped my shoulder and waited to fly. I moved to my post, hands gripping the reins. My eyes found Graham adjusting his tack one last time. He spoke with his opposing teammate and friend Austin, his hands moving the latigo with ease and familiarity. They were smiling, even laughing, and I knew they were exchanging words in friendly mockery. It was their way to calm each other.

Our horses clumped together in herd-like behavior, many of their hips donning initials of a man, a brand, forever melted into them. Ray Ely was as cowboy as they came, the belt buckle big and shiny against his small frame. A Stetson, white, sharp and shaped perfectly was most at home atop his head. Blue wranglers, clean and starched, bore a circular mark worn into his back pocket. He used to hide his can there, spitting in secret.

Ranching life was not always easy on Ray as lines weaved deep into a face written with stories of adventure, quests and escapades. If only everyone could experience what he had during his lifetime. But there had been hard times too—ones he was forced to live through, to suffer through. Hard work made them pass, and faith made him a better man, a better husband, a better father. In the end, life had been worth it.

His experience, skill and wisdom were unmatched. No one could doctor a horse quite like Ray, and he knew his horses better than anyone. He was a good man, an even better horseman.

His ranch boasted horses like Crockett, born, bred and raised with a desire to continue a legacy through them for years to come. But Crockett's hip was a clean slate, falling into Graham's hands before the hot iron brand could touch him.

That day a few years back, the heat was so thick it was hard to breathe. The sun's relentless rays beat my back while I taught and instructed the little ones, horses circling and turning around cones and over ground rails. I will never forget how Ray's aging body scampered over the wooden rails with Graham walking right beside:

"You like that there colt Graham?" His weathered hand rested on a dark mare. The blood bay foal carefully positioned himself to eat, pushing and sucking aggressively, milk dripping from wrinkled lips. The foal took in the men sheepishly, too busy to take much notice. Other mares with foals munched and broke hay, oblivious.

"He's a nice colt, Ray."

"He's yours then." A stunned Graham reached for Ray's extended hand to finalize it. With that, the colt came to us, and we named him Crockett after Graham's grandmother's horse—the one she rode as a small girl through the Texas heat to school.

When all the other horses headed back to Missouri for the long winter months, Crockett stayed with his fuzzy coat. His colt fur eventually fell out, and his true blood color deep and dark and red unveiled itself. It took time for him to grow big enough. And in the meantime, we waited patiently, dreaming of the day he would be strong enough to hold someone.

As he grew, my responsibilities quickly transitioned, and I soon took over Ray's horsemanship program. Ray and his wife

Louise had run it for years, and I took on the challenge. I was responsible for everything—every child and horse. And I could not let them down. Their lessons were invaluable. Louise's feisty mentality and steadfastness in decisions quickly rubbed off on me as I worked my way into their shoes, which were hard to fill. But I did my best.

A few years later, Louise met Jesus in Heaven, and Ray joined her soon after. Their hard work was forever an example to me, and their greatest gift was that horse for my husband.

Music drifting through black speakers brought me back to the present, and lights sprung awake to illuminate the entire arena. A familiar song began to play. Our horses noticed with pricking ears. The announcer atop his favorite introduced the sport of rodeo, galloping quickly to exit when he had done his duty. It was our turn.

Moving as one, we funneled through a creaking wooden gate and separated—some right, some left forming two groups. Lines traced the outer edges of the arena, slowly at first but quickly picking up speed. Flags flew high. We loped past crowds holding babies, popcorn, hamburgers, and balloons. Finally crossing each other and facing the audience, flashes popped and sprung before us.

I steadied neatly next to Graham, so close our knees touched. I smiled at him, and he smiled back—his flushed face clear and etching itself deep in my memory. I would never love anyone like I love him.

Silence accompanied the stars and stripes on horseback—you couldn't even hear the hooves traveling around, lost in the deep soil. The flag whipped with force, seeming to sing its own version of the National Anthem. Voices rose and hands crossed hearts out of respect—one of my favorite parts of the night. We left the arena fast with the dust rising behind us.

Our dog Ivy helped in the team-penning event. Her body lowered easily to the ground like a snake creeping in the hunt, the prey a group of steer moving carelessly around the arena. The crowds gasped as she came within just inches of being kicked or trampled. Cow-sense breeding was the only thing keeping her alive. After her show, she scurried to me, anticipating praise, which came in the form of cool water rushing over her tongue and body. She was proud of her work, as was I.

She bounded alongside me eager to rest in the horse trailer where Graham met us, always willing to help.

"Need me to put her away?" He strode alongside, his chaps brushing each other with swooshing sounds.

"I can handle her. You have to go." I was halfway to my destination.

Graham moved in the direction of the arena, readying himself for steer roping.

I heaved the heavy metal door open and hurried Ivy into the cave-like home. She sank into hay and sleep. With a creak, I moved the door shut, locked and secure. I raced to a spot on the rail, anxious to watch.

There he was, swinging easily onto Crockett, lasso hung casually on the horn. Rope and hand met like an old married couple, and he unwound a small loop testing its flexibility. Warming it up, he moved Crockett forward toward the iron gates. Graham in blue, Austin in red, they waited for the announcer to introduce them. Swinging gates slowly opened allowing them entrance. With a click, they were in. No turning back now. Friends fighting for the chance to lasso one steer, release it and lasso another for the victory. Jaws tightened and legs fought to stand still under saddle.

The group of steers stood at the far end of the arena. Sticking together was their only option—their possibility of safety. Tails swished at flies, and noses dripped a clear fluid. Long sticky tongues wiped it away.

Loping as a pair, the riders set out toward the herd, talking one last time, poking fun. It was inevitable now. The time had come.

Austin set right to work, separating out a black bovine easily. He moved closer and readied his rope for the job. Swinging quickly, he released his chance only to come up short. The cow moved away free. Dragging the lasso back to his horse, he recoiled his loop and regrouped for another shot.

Attention moved to Graham who caught sight of a red steer that had challenged him earlier in the weekly practice. Graham, attracted to his wild and fast ways, set out to conquer him once again. There was something bigger than even horse and rider drawing them all together. It was simply meant to be. Working methodically, Graham moved the cow away from the herd. Crockett locked eyes like a hunter tracking the trail of rising dust. His duty was obvious.

I watched, my heart pumping out a rhythm matching the speed of the race—my knuckles pale on the rail. My husband's calm demeanor, a show of confident quiet, fascinated me. His loop began lifting to the night sky held by his strong right hand— reins and coil in the other. Growing and spinning faster, the loop circled above. In all the roughness of sport, the lasso flew with grace and precision like that of his fly-fishing line casting across the clear waters of our river. Catching a spooky trout or a quick cow drove a passion inside him that even I couldn't understand. It didn't matter that hundreds were watching and waiting; it was only horse, rider and cow on this night. They straightened themselves down the arena.

Crockett matched his victim, and with it Graham unknowingly surrendered his rope and life to the plans set out before him. Like an arm reaching out, the mark was hit in perfect formation, wrapping the neck and drawing tight. Hands with finger-like fibers clutched the throat. He had him. A dally to the horn secured the plot.

I blinked, a cheer rising in my throat, ready to escape. Crockett slowed to bring the beast down. Upon feeling the rope, the red bullet darted sharply to the right and set the stage. My cheer would remain forever trapped inside me. Crockett tried to react to the shift in events, his legs working hard to balance in the middle of the momentum. He wasn't expecting this. Distorting and giving way beneath himself, he had no choice. He was falling. Legs tried desperately to sturdy themselves and remain strong, but it was no use. He positioned himself for the somersault. I cringed at the thought of broken legs.

Graham held tight to the reins, perhaps mostly out of reflex. Nonetheless, he prevented Crockett from flipping. Crashing however was inevitable, and I watched helplessly as the precious horse and my beloved husband slammed into the arena floor. The exact cause and effect was unknown to me, but I would never forget the vivid picture of my husband's head whiplashing against earth. It bounced like a ball only to land again, finding a resting place in the dirt. The picture was seared into my mind.

I waited a fraction of a second but saw only stillness. My body hurled itself between the rails, desperate. Dust lifted, as did my heavy legs. Crowds gasped and rose as one, watching quietly. I wasn't sure if I could make it. My breathing was so shallow.

"Lord, help me!" It was all I could get out.

He met me there. Strong legs, not my own, took me back to a path lined with pine trees I once raced as a child—the Dark Stretch. His legs carried me at that moment to my husband.

I found Graham on his side, eerily quiet—caked in dirt and still as if in death. I knelt by him, about to tug and pull his stocky frame toward me. Breath reached his lungs, but the sound was not right. Snoring and rasping pierced my ears. I touched the dirty face, realizing his cowboy hat had been thrown about 20 feet from the scene. I waited for a response, anything to give hope. Crockett lay still, stunned from the impact.

The steer, free from his captor, raised itself and trotted to the safety of the herd. The lasso clung to his neck.

"Graham!" I was certain my voice would do the trick and awaken the snoring slumber. Austin appeared instantly above us—face tense, red shirt bright with life. He slowly worked his way to remove Graham's foot that was caught deep in the stirrup. It jerked free and with it Crockett, eyes glazed over, rose slowly from his spot in the dust. He was sturdy on four legs, no broken bones.

To horse, something was amiss. The glazed look replaced itself with panic and eyes began lining with white—a clear sign he knew something was terribly wrong.

Roping reins drooped loose across his neck. No direction or guidance from Graham could leave him to his own demise. Crockett's breast collar, snapped and dangling in front of his legs swung back and forth slowly like the arm of a grandfather clock. Alarmed and scared, he began to move. One step, then two. His pulling revealed Graham's other boot caught in the stirrup fastening Graham like a seat belt to the horse. Graham's body began to slide.

"Get his foot out!" I clung to his frame, willing him not to go. I couldn't reach the stirrup.

Lunging and thinking fast, Austin knocked him free, his leg landing on the ground with a thud. Graham lay completely still, unaware through it all. Led away by waiting hands, Crockett left the chaos quickly unfolding.

Before I knew it, a lady from the crowd was holding Graham's head and talking to him. I gripped his shoulders. No blood. No bones evading his body. He slept, eyes shut. I wanted to force them open. *Wake up. Please wake up.*

His thigh trembled under the stress—my heart clenched in fear.

My sister Bonnie reached me and without words bent to take Graham's pulse. I was pulled away, hands and arms holding me at bay, allowing the first responders room. Steady fingers removed the blue fabric, cutting at an angle. A blood pressure cuff wrapped his right arm while oxygen smothered his face, a small green tank sat next to him.

I was numb and although surrounded by many, alone and cold. I saw myself standing there, at the beginning of a path I wasn't sure I wanted to travel. It was pine laden, raw with branches and calling my name. I couldn't run. Or even turn. I had to face this Dark Stretch. Alone.

The sirens met my ears and pulled me back to reality. Prayers seeped through the loud speakers, pleading for Graham's life. The crowds continued to watch. Helpless. All we could do was pray. I felt them and treasured their intent.

Applause erupted, and an ambulance moved through the gates. It struggled only slightly in the turned up soil.

The head EMT shook her head, radio in hand.

"We need a helicopter. This won't do!" She barked out orders. I watched her take control and message into her walkie talkie.

"It can land in the arena." Another EMT reported.

"We can't stop transport." The small lady argued. "We'll be en route to another landing station." She returned full attention back to Graham.

An orange backboard appeared, stiff and uninviting, along with a small bag. Blocks, straps and other materials landed, open and clean. Hands grabbed each piece, eager to put them in their proper place. It reminded me of the puzzles I liked to do as a small child, each piece carefully fit and placed exactly right. He rolled easily onto the board, experienced arms holding him secure. Sleep remained, eyes locked, plastered in dirt.

Like a spider's web, straps spun themselves along his body bolting him tight. His neck was unable to move. A stretcher rolled by and lowered itself for easy lifting. Things were moving fast.

My sister reassured me he'd be okay. I looked deeper into her eyes. She was a nurse. She was lying to me. Always the one prepared, she slipped a fifty into my pocket and hugged me. My brother, Matt, followed right behind. He ran from the arena. The boys would be okay with mom, and dad was on his way. I raced for the ambulance afraid it would leave me. I took one last look at Graham—loaded into the back, doors slamming behind him.

I pulled a metal handle and scurried in. Lights bounced off the hood of the ambulance.

We started moving, sirens screaming. I wanted to scream too. We drove away from the applauding crowds left to wonder what was to come.

More clothing was ripped and cut landing precariously on the aluminum floor. IV's pushed their way through veins. Saline bags hung overhead.

"Graham." They repeated his name. Nothing. His bare legs bounced from the speed and bumps in the road.

It was dark, our beams the only thing lighting the way. We rode quickly as the EMTs battled to stay balanced.

With heart beating fast, I watched. *Where was he? Where was my husband?*

I shook at the picture before me.

"Have you noticed my servant, Graham?"

"He is a fine man, blameless and of complete integrity. He fears God and stays away from evil."

My eyes stung, playing the story.

"Yes, because *You* have protected him. *You* have made him prosper in everything he does. Look how blessed he is!"

I knew the coming reply. It pierced my heart like a dagger driving deep.

"All right, you may test him. His wife too."

The Dark Stretch I remembered as a child was right in front of me. I had to move forward. I could not waiver any longer. Would I answer as Job did?

"I came naked from my mother's womb, and I will be naked when I leave. The Lord gave me what I had and the Lord has taken it away. Praise the name of the Lord!"

A familiar old logging road loomed in front of me where my training as a young rider was tested. Horse and I racing as one.

It was right there. I could almost feel the branches scraping my skin, the sound of the hooves quick and traveling fast. Would I make it to the end this time? A victor? A champion? Or would I stumble to the hard and unforgiving ground? I was being swallowed whole. The Dark Stretch my captor.

2
RACING PONIES

'The sight of that pony did something to me I've never quite been able to explain. He was more than tremendous strength and speed and beauty and motion. He set me dreaming.'
~Walt Morey

It was a quick season, but it had been beautiful, alive. The leaves peaked slowly to start it all bursting thick at the peak: the middle of summer. Bright colors during brisk mornings now splashed the land. This was their encore, their final act. And it was too short. The now pale leaf broke free from its perch, finally succumbing to its death. It floated carefully to the ground, resting on my boot. Shaking it off, I listened for the crunch, my foot smashing it into dirt. Several others followed suit dripping like soft rain. I wound my way along the path to their house, determined not to meet the same fate as the leaves. Today I would stand my ground. I wouldn't be crushed.

I was almost there, the blonde heads, one just a bit taller than the other matched my pace. I breathed in big, ready. My young 9-year-old body, usually tall and wiry, seemed small today, almost frail.

"You came!" The younger sister broke free, her legs covering the distance between us quickly. She wanted to welcome me in, but my face made her hesitate.

She stopped, eyebrows raised. Only one question filled her mind.

"You're not going to do it are you?"

My hands clenched at my side. "I can't." I waited, my breath holding tight in my throat. The sisters looked at each other, then back at me.

"You won't get any better always riding in a saddle." The older sister, almost 12, spoke now. Her gaze held no sympathy for me. I stared at them both, unwilling to yield.

"Okay, let's go." They both turned, it was their way of respecting my wishes. I followed close behind, my embarrassment lasting only moments.

We reached the electric fence. The ticking buzz was a constant reminder not to touch the hot silver wire. Encountered before, the lesson was never forgotten. By now we knew what to do.

Lowering our bodies we were under in seconds to leave behind the world of most girls our age. Fingernails lined with dirt. Pants with holes from past adventures. Boots scraped through the terrain, caring not when meeting the squishy sounds of manure and mud. We couldn't explain what we craved here. We just had to have it. And we were never satisfied.

We were childhood friends, sharing more than just secrets and promises. Katie, the eldest, was determined to prove herself. Driven by desires deep within her, I never asked, I simply followed. There was never any reason to doubt her leadership, her rightful place as the eldest. Somehow she had all the answers we'd ever need; her experience and knowledge was good enough for us. Her silky hair was pulled back today, hanging in a perfectly formed braid down her back. It was long and so blonde it looked white. Her smile was straight, her nose just the right size. She still held onto her childhood innocence, although it wouldn't be for much longer.

Karrie, a similar picture of her sister physically, was quite different in other ways. Quiet and shy, she was like a small flower struggling to bloom and conform to those around her. Her confidence would come with time; those closest to her knew this. She was my most loyal friend. It had been this way since diapers and burp cloths. No one knew each other like we did. And we were certain it would stay this way. Our differences drew us together, working perfectly. We didn't need to say much to know. We just understood. We had nothing to prove. Nothing to show. We were just us with our water and oil personalities. She was the smallest of our group but easily the bravest. She couldn't be shown up. She would not get left behind. Her agile body, while small, could do things mine wouldn't dream of doing. I knew better than to challenge her, compete against her. She'd always win. Or die trying. I learned early on I couldn't beat her. So, I joined her instead, always taking her side. Always on her team.

Our youthful legs brought us to a small red tack shed in the middle of a large corral. The silver fencing stretched beyond what we could see. With a lift of a wooden latch and a pull of a door we stepped up and into a place of rawhide and leather. Soft blankets draped worn saddles, and trunks of supplies rested comfortably, lids secure and tight. Bridles hung carefully on hooks, waiting and ready. Dust danced in the sun-streamed room, our bodies forcing it to find a new place to float and roam. I coughed some out.

We rummaged and sorted. Parts of a saddle small enough for pony and me began coming together: a fleece girth, billets, stirrups. Multi-colored pony halters hung on a nail nearby, lead ropes already attached. We each grabbed one, mine nestling between fingers and palm. We left the rigged up saddle near the door and made our way to the horses.

"Now the hard part." Katie confessed. Her eyes scanned the area looking for the small herd. Mine did the same.

There they were. Together in some trees trying their best to hide. Eyes locked on us like a gun's scope following our every move. Who was doing the hunting had not yet been determined.

"Wait here." Katie moved forward, her arm cocked awkwardly; a bright red halter hid itself behind her back. She was trying her best to hide the ultimate goal of the capture. The ponies continued to stand staring, almost inviting her in. We knew their tricks just as they knew ours. Waiting, they allowed her a few steps, eyes following her every move. For a moment, I thought we wouldn't have to work for our ride. I was quickly proven wrong. Like a whistle blown, or a line crossed too far, they broke as one. Heads held high in defiance. Tails like flags raised in a challenge. They were flying right toward us.

Their legs rumbled and whizzed past us, taunting us on their way by. We were left with no choice. And so the chase began. The two white ponies galloped around a small pond with the brown one close behind. Clumps of dirt kicked up in our faces as we sprung forward, our breath working hard to keep up.

We were somewhat smarter than the equines. And having done this a time or two before, a plan quickly came together. A small pen, which was used to grain and separate some of the horses, opened. Karrie worked the gate while standing on the bottom rung riding it to its end. She would wait patiently for her cue.

My hand continued to clutch halter and lead. It was no longer necessary to keep it hidden. I headed up the wings of the operation and helped cut off the party as best I could. I followed the commands given me. With patience and determination we teased and worked them into the pen, the gate swinging quickly behind. It locked shut, and we breathed a bit easier with the job now more attainable. Although they were not yet caught, the space they had to run was small—too small to get away. I leaned on the gate to catch my breath. The sisters did the same as we watched them for a moment.

Their display of displeasure was obvious as they pranced and danced about, clearly trying to intimidate. Heads tossed, manes flapped and front legs sparred for the imaginary joust. Eyes no longer watched but rather avoided, hoping to be forgotten and left behind.

Their round bellies were too large to continue the tirade for long. Laziness soon won out. We climbed the fence, ready for the final act, our own lungs recouped. They knew what awaited them and feeling the defeat of battle, their heads lowered. Submission the only option, they breathed deep, nostrils flared pink from the workout.

The ringleader, a pure white pony named, Sugar, was anything but sweet. She stood slightly in front of the other two, daring us to slip the red nylon over her nose.

But Katie took her challenge.

The white coat accompanied with a full mane and tail gave the impression of safety and fun memories. She was the kind you picture little girls climbing onto, trotting around a brick house without fear, safely carrying her passengers. Her eyes told a much different story, her past evident within them.

It wasn't her fault she was like this. It wasn't the blonde sisters either. Her world had been jerked and pulled into something she only wanted to fight and resist. She had been forced too far. As a result, she was spoiled and sour. But now she was here with these sisters. She was beginning to find peace. Trust was just starting to form.

Moving with confidence, Katie walked forward talking quietly to the mare. Ears moved forward and back, torn between two voices. In front was the girl's voice, sweet and comforting. Behind her was a voice only she could hear, begging her to run and flee again. It was familiar to her. Karrie and I watched, waiting for her decision.

Her answer came with the lift of a hoof, a step in the right direction. Nose reached out, and Katie's soft fingers stroked short hairs. Hands rubbed themselves along the thick neck and the halter moved into place. It snapped. Katie continued rubbing.

Karrie and I leapt from our spots as one. We reached the other two without trouble and soon had them trailing behind. We once again headed to the tack shed.

Curry combs and soft brushes rubbed and massaged, blowing hair and dust into the air. Perhaps the birds would find this treasure of hair in the spring, their young resting in comfort against the softness.

I continued the task before me, rubbing back, girth line and many other places on the small grey and white gelding. The ponies were now at ease. This ritual from the brush felt good to them. Places were scratched that they couldn't reach causing them to breathe deep with pleasure.

I threw the blanket with pad. The saddle followed close behind. The girth swung in anticipation, and I grabbed it easily
resting it behind the front legs. A latigo knot soon formed, and I
placed the small snaffle bit into the warm mouth. We were just
about ready.

"I don't know if it's going to stay." Katie grabbed the horn
and rocked the saddle from side to side to test its placement and
durability. It was a sorry sight.

"It'll stay." Karrie was growing impatient. She leapt up onto
the brown pony with one easy, fluid motion. Unlike me, she rode
bareback. The pony, impatient too, started walking away. Karrie
found her seat just in time.

"It's fine." I reassured Katie. I could tell she didn't like the
looks of the saddle. She shrugged her shoulders and left to hop
onto Sugar. There was no saddle for her either.

I gripped the horn and placed my foot in the stirrup. I found
my way up and plopped down. Though not as adventurous as
the sisters, I felt safe. I was certain they were the crazy ones, but
their experience was evident as they melted into their ponies and
moved as one. I couldn't help but be jealous.

Within minutes we were completely hidden in the Adirondack Mountains and woods. It was our home. We could ride and
explore as far as we dared to let the hooves take us. No one knew
we were here.

In the summer the mountains were lush and green. Their
thick branches and trunks coated the hills and rocks making it
easy to hide, which we often did. Childhood adventures tempted
and prodded the seclusion we could only get in these woods. It
was coolest here, the trees blocking and shielding us from the
hot summer sun. We were good at disappearing from every

responsibility and chore awaiting us at home. We were experts at imagining and pretending.

The ever-changing leaves opened and closed the mountains like a treasure chest revealing its secrets and mysteries. A curtain pulled back each year for us to peer behind making the fall my favorite time to be here. She seemed vulnerable, her scars evident and easily seen. But, the 4,000-foot peaks were devious and anything but vulnerable. Still, we liked to think we were invincible within her walls, that she'd protect us, look after us.

The winters were ruthless, long and uncaring. It didn't matter that we lived here, that we called this place home. This kind of nature thought nothing of our safety or well-being. We were left to battle out the snowstorms time after time. It was simply the way of life.

We weren't natives. Only those surviving third or fourth generations claimed that status. We were only locals, but we were proud of it. Weathered, simple and loyal to our own, we accepted that our town depended much on tourists to survive. Our draw? Schroon Lake, nestled in the mountains just like many others and providing endless past times to those able to partake.

Her size breathtaking, her beauty drawing them in like a child to a decorated Christmas tree, she was and is respected as the matriarch. She helps us survive here. A river, the lake's little sister, extends as an arm, feeding life into the older ones' mouth, providing fuel and supply.

This river, north of her big sister, found its way along our homes. Her waters were clear and inviting in the dry, hot summers. We danced on her banks and swam in her cool waters, rope swings dangling above. Dark and icy waters in the spring forced us to wait, hopeful for a day to play again. We would always come back to her. And like a dependable friend, she was always there waiting.

"Let's run!" Karrie took off without another word, soft clumps of dirt kicking up behind her.

I hardly had time to ready myself, my pony wanting to join. Katie was not to be beaten and easily began chasing her sister down the narrow path. They were so competitive. And stubborn. Impossible to beat.

I had no choice but to keep up, my pony making all the decisions. His short legs clipped through the leaves and dirt, his neck stretched out. I let him run.

The excitement built as we continued on, trying to pass each other, the feat difficult to accomplish on such a pass as this. Our laughter was loud, and we listened for the wind to carry them away. The ponies persisted on, fresh and full of new spunk despite their big bellies. I felt free. Nothing could touch me. Or so I thought.

The safety net and anchor to the grey pony began swaying from side to side. I looked down, watching muscles quiver and work to keep up. My eyes caught the girth coming undone from the speed and poor fit. A hand could fit between it and the horse easily. It was clear: I was atop a ticking bomb about to go off.

My pony sensed the danger as well. The freedom I felt I deserved was quickly spreading to panic as the reality of my situation sunk in. I would soon fall.

My screams went unnoticed from the back. The other ponies continued on without a care, my own keeping up, almost bumping into the other's legs and hocks. I attempted to balance myself, but it was difficult as the saddle bounced and rocked precariously. It became apparent gravity was going to win out.

My glances caused the final blow. My body couldn't sustain the saddle any longer; it began slipping to the right. I found myself with no other option but to bail into a thick patch of bushes. I could only hope for the best.

The saddle found a new home under the pony, the girth now resting above its back. I watched from my place on the ground as the sorry pair continued running. The pony was distressed, running faster than I had ever seen him go. He easily passed the other two and darted into the woods.

The sisters pulled their ponies to a halt. Katie leapt from Sugar and threw her reins to Karrie quickly, almost like she had practiced it. Karrie held tight and waited.

I stood to my feet, brushing sticks and leaves from my clothing. A few scratches were all I sustained on my way down.

I watched the sisters. They remained calm and sure as they quickly caught and released my pony from the trap of the saddle. It fell to the ground with a thud. Relieved, I started walking to the group.

"You okay?" Karrie tried to sound sympathetic. It was no use; her face quickly broke into a smile. Her cheeks flushed red.

We all laughed, aware of how pathetic I looked.

"Now, you have no choice but to ride bareback." Katie rested the saddle and pads at the edge of the trail, her hands already forming a step to give me a boost up.

I knew the moment had come. It was time to break away from the confines of the saddle. Today was the day. I sighed heavily, the sisters both staring at me, prodding me on.

"Okay." I walked to the pony and bent my knee for the mount. I grabbed some mane and waited.

Katie easily threw me up and over, my legs resting against the soft hair. I clutched the reins and continued to grip the mane with all my might.

"Just relax Randi, you'll get it."

I tried to relax. But it was hard. We started moving once again. I glanced around nervously, waiting for anything and everything to spook my pony and send me to the ground once again.

But nothing happened. I was actually staying on.

Gentle chatter and a slow walk calmed my nerves. I too began to melt into the pony, my legs and body moving as they should. A smile soon began to replace my panicked look. We began to trot. I didn't fall. We worked into a lope. I stayed put. We were laughing once again, my own loudest of all. Now I truly was free.

We continued to wind in and out of brush and trees, our destination unspoken, but clearly known by both our ponies and us. We were being sucked in once again. And we were fine with that.

It was narrow, the place we called 'The Dark Stretch'. We had named the old logging road ourselves. And the name fit perfectly, encased by dense pine trees, giving off an eerie feel even in the middle of a bright day. It was just wide enough for a small car to drive through, making it an ideal place for a race.

We were fortunate never to have gotten hurt or killed doing what we loved to do. We would bet, and we would compete, and we didn't always play nice. Bridles were pulled off during the battle to the finish, and ponies were spooked and teased. We did what we had to do to crown a new champion for the day.

The ponies had learned early on that the path was only passed with speed and flight. This first glimpse of darkness coming toward them was the green flag whipping in the wind, cueing us to go whether we were ready or not. A fistful of mane secured our place in the crazy flight of hooves. We were born to do this. Something inside drove us, pushing us to race. Any fear or trepidation was forced elsewhere because today was no different than any other. Today we would race. And at the end of it, we all hoped to cross the unmarked line first.

3
SAVE THE BELT BUCKLE

'You never know how much you really believe anything until its truth or falsehood becomes a matter of life and death to you.'
~ C.S. Lewis

It came for him, buzzing and hovering over my head like a bumblebee. Smaller than I thought it should be, the helicopter landed and waited for its unconscious cargo. I wondered where they would fit him. One pilot sat in his seat at the front, his head-gear secure and tight. He looked serious, experienced. He had done this a time or two before. The other stood quietly talking to a firefighter, his jumpsuit a dark blue and zipped up to his chin, a patch or two sewn into the rough fabric perhaps carrying his name, his rank.

Other firefighters stood nearby in their worn yellow suits. They had to be hot in the heavy gear and summer heat. Complete strangers all here to lend their services, talents, time.

I was afraid to look into the ambulance. Against my hearts' wishes, my feet walked me to the back. Perhaps in those few seconds of walking, things would change. I hoped it to be true. I was ready to peer back into the terror when my eyes caught movement headed my way.

It was my father.

I moved toward him; his legs covered the distance between us in no time. He must have gotten a call. He must have rushed here. Relief flooded my being. My dad would know what to do, how to fix this.

I cried in his arms, and he held me strong. I could feel some of his own fear as he saw for the first time the severity of the situation. I knew in an instant he could do nothing.

There was no more scurrying about and frantic radio calls. Even with so many, it remained quiet. Eerily so.

I watched, wrapped in my father's arms as the EMTs readied to shove a plastic tube down Graham's throat. I knew what was about to happen. And I couldn't watch.

We were pulled away from the scene once again, and I stole a look at Graham before they loaded him into the helicopter. So still, unmoving. His bare feet hung over the stretcher. He would've loved to go for a ride in that helicopter. Too bad he wasn't going to remember it.

We were forced to head south, traveling to a hospital that could handle his injuries. I made a phone call. Indiana and his father seemed a world away. We cried. He prayed with me. His own mind had to be racing, filled with those horrible memories he had similar to this when his wife was taken from him. Would he be losing his son tonight?

Arriving at the hospital, we were ushered into a room. It was more like a holding cell; all I wanted to do was break free and find him. A few chairs lined one side of the wall while an old, worn-out couch squared off with them. They attempted to welcome me but fell quite short. The walls coiled around me like vines clinging to their host. I could almost hear the weeping from news heard not so long ago. Would I be just another participant? Another body folded in the cushions crying for my loved one? I stood waiting, my pastor and his wife already with us. Their faces strained as if braced for the worse. I couldn't sit.

A social worker and priest were there almost instantly. Her eyes moved to find me. The wife. The one left with the questions, the fear. She didn't hesitate. She wouldn't keep me waiting.

"I'm so sorry for your loss." She seemed sincerely sorry for me. My eyes immediately jumped to my dad who stood perplexed and shocked. I reached behind me for the arm of the chair. It was finally time to sink down into it.

"No one has told us he is dead yet. Are you sure you have the right person?"

My dad fumbled over his words. Shock clearly evident.

"Oh, I'm so sorry. I was given information that he….." she was trailing off quickly, embarrassed for her possible mistake.

"Well, can you make sure?" My pastor asked this, desperate for answers. Something in his voice propelled her out the door even faster.

I felt numb, my stomach nauseous. I almost didn't want her to come back for fear of what news would accompany her.

Lord, please don't let him be dead yet; I didn't even get to say goodbye.

The priest, still standing in the room with us, clutched his Bible, his large eyes darting around the room. He wasn't uneasy. He wasn't pushy. He was just there. And he was oddly comfortable with all this.

News finally did arrive. Graham remained asleep, still alive. A CAT scan was working hard to find answers. And in the meantime, the mood in the holding cell started to come alive.

Friends came to be with me. Most had been at the rodeo. They had seen what happened just hours before and made the long trip to encourage me. I couldn't believe the support. Even in my dazed, confused and nauseous state, I was grateful.

My mind began to slow as the numbing agent of my husband's injury worked its way into my body. My responses became hollow like I was witnessing myself saying them. My movements even took on a whole new feeling. Swallowing took extreme concentration. Moving my hand to my lap felt weird. I concluded I had to be experiencing a nightmare. The only problem was, I kept repeating in my brain to "WAKE UP!" But it just wouldn't.

I have always been a dreamer. Graham called mine "movie dreams" because most were so detailed it was like I was in a movie or at least watching one. He'd love to hear all about them the morning after. He'd sit like a small schoolboy ready for the adventure of his life while I replayed my night of battles, cool stunts and embarrassing moments to him. He was always jealous that I dreamed so much. But no matter what he did or ate, he just didn't dream.

The minutes in the room ticked on without word. We prayed. We waited.

We prayed some more. We talked. We laughed. We cried. By now, hours had passed since Graham's fall. I started to get antsy.

What is going on? Why can't I see him for a minute just to know he's okay?

Then it came. That summon you know you should obey but a big part of you doesn't want to, afraid of the outcome, the result awaiting you. I rose and started toward those double doors that would begin my journey of medical jargon, doctors, nurses and the aspect that was the most troubling of all. The waiting.

I made it through the doors with my dad gripping my arm so tight it hurt. An ER doctor met us. She looked young. Her red hair was surprisingly pretty and well done for a busy doctor such as herself. I wanted to keep moving, to get to him, but she blocked my way. She was talking to me. She reminded me of those commercials on TV where the words don't quite match the persons' lips and all you want to do is fix it. It wasn't her mistake. It was that numbing agent still pounding through my veins, slowing my brain.

"We just got done reading the CAT scan, but we won't know the full extent of his injuries until we do an MRI."

My dad, my brother, and myself waited for more. We were frozen, unable to move even if we dared.

"He has quite a bruise on the right side of his brain, along with some bleeding that has started. His back is broken, and we don't know yet about his spinal cord. His neck seems fine, but his back and brain have us somewhat concerned at this point. We have him lightly sedated, but he's still not responding to any stimulus from us. We will simply have to wait and see."

"We're working on getting him into a room up in the Intensive Care Unit. At this time, there are none available so he'll have to stay here." She pointed to a room directly off to the side of her. I didn't want to hear anymore. I knew where I was going now.

Seeing the one you promised your life to for the first time after something like this happens is heart wrenching. He was strapped up to so many tubes it was hard to make him out. But it was him alright. Those hands once held mine tightly, tempting me to play thumb wars in the most inconvenient of places: church, weddings, serious meetings. I picked one up. So limp. I could easily beat him now.

Breath worked its way in and out of him through the tube down his throat. He looked more relaxed than before, probably from the catheter in his arm pumping from the bag hanging just above him. A face that started the night clean was covered in dust, which found its way into the creases of his forehead, his nose and around his mouth. I looked more closely. His teeth brown, his clothes shredded on the floor nearby. They must have taken them from the ambulance. A dusty film lay on the once white tiles. We all stood in it. I snatched his belt and belt buckle from the counter. At least those could be saved. A nurse forced me to slip off the one piece of jewelry he had, his wedding band, silver, thick and well worn from his finger. It didn't want to come.

A thin white sheet covered his body while a heat lamp poured what it could offer on him. I kissed his forehead. His smell was just as I remembered it to always be. But then I heard the noises: the beeping of the machines behind him, the slight gurgling sounds from that thin tube down his nose, the inflating and deflating of the blood pressure cuff. I couldn't let my ears take it all in. I simply held fast to his hand, waiting for it to move. It was impossible not to let my mind wander down a road I never thought it would have to.

Is he paralyzed? Is he going to wake up? Oh Lord, please, don't take him from me yet.

He met me once again. Right there in that ER room. It was soft. It was comforting.

I AM with you.

I sat or stood the rest of the night holding that same hand. It was difficult. And I had no idea how much more difficult it was going to get. If I knew, perhaps I would have wept. I definitely would have screamed. But none of that came for me. I was scared out of my mind, but something else was happening, something that can never fully be explained. I was handed for the first time in my life exactly what I needed to get through only each new minute that came ticking my way. Before, I would've pouted. I would've thrown a fit. It didn't seem fair to have control over only one minute at a time. But I tried to see it as it was. A gift—a special gift from the Lord.

By 4 a.m., it was apparent nothing magical was happening. Thoughts of a simple concussion were dashed. Nurses came and went, checking the hanging bags above, looking at the screens behind him. A room finally did open up for him. I wondered who could've died. What family was crying now? They wheeled him out and up to the ICU floor. A whole new world awaited me there—one I didn't particularly like.

I would eventually have to give in to sleep. My body never did well staying up late. It'd be shutting down soon. I was that girl at the slumber parties who always fell asleep first. I'd awaken to silly stuffed animals around my head, positioned just right. I was certain to be the laughing stock of any overnight party. Maybe that's why I was always invited. When I was young and out with my family, I'd climb under an end table to sleep. They'd eventually find me and carry me home. Even as a baby, I loved to sleep. My mother was often forced to check on me to make sure I was still breathing.

I slept hard that morning in a motor home parked in a parking lot near the hospital. So much was happening behind the scenes. The placement of this haven for me was just one of the many blessings that would follow. My phone said 8 a.m. when I finally hit the bed in the back. But my body only allowed a little sleep. I jumped awake at 10 a.m. still running on adrenaline.

Certain he'd be awake, staring around the room, joking with the nurses, I raced for his bed. That would be just like him, trying to make this funny. The scene I came upon was much different than the one I pictured in my head.

The dirt on his face and body had been wiped clean, doctors bending over his bed. His nurse stood in the background, waiting, watching the monitors. A notebook rested in her hands as she documented every number, line and shape from the machines parked behind him.

What are they doing to him? They allowed me to stay. I should've left.

A shiny object caught my attention in the hands of one. A hemostat. I waited.

"GRAHAM, CAN YOU HEAR US? CAN YOU MOVE YOUR HAND IF YOU CAN HEAR US?"

It was ridiculously loud. They waited.

There was no response. And that's when one grabbed his hand, the left one. Gripping it, I assumed they would squeeze it for a response. Instead the hemostat dug itself into his pointer fingernail. No reaction. This continued through all the fingers on that hand including his thumb. Each time the hemostat dug a bit harder, a bit stronger. The doctors' own hands shook from the strain of pushing down. Nothing.

They moved to the right hand and continued again. Nothing. Nobody wanted those fingers to move more than I did. But still, they lay limp.

I thought they were done, that they would leave him alone. They didn't. Grabbing a clump of chest hair with some skin, they pinched and twisted for a response. It was apparent he was feeling nothing. My mouth filled with cotton. Some more tests were done on his toes, inner thighs and arms. Bruises would soon appear, purple, blue, yellow.

A gaze met from across Graham's body. It was the kind you wish you hadn't seen from doctor to doctor as they inaudibly discuss the problems awaiting them, awaiting the family.

I leaned forward hoping they'd have some answers. I couldn't believe he was still asleep.

Didn't he just bump his head a little?

"We will have to wait and see." With that, they vanished. An hour went by before the whole process started up again. I accepted it. I told myself it was necessary. This time, however, I left.

I knew what I had to do. And couldn't wait any longer. I dug around for someone's cell phone and made the call.

I couldn't say much. The emotion in my throat caught my words pulling them away like a mother grabbing her young child away from the edge of a pool. But, they still needed to know their son was not waking up.

In a few short hours, his parents were on their way. The next day they were there.

4
COOL RIVER SWIM

And so I write this for you, My Sarah. With the hope that one day, when you're old enough, this story that lives with me, will live with you as well. When a story is told, it is not forgotten. It becomes something else, a memory of who we were; the hope of what we can become.
~ Julia Jarmond from Sarah's Key.

Ours was the kind you're supposed to remember. It should be burned in the mind and heart: the first meeting. But somehow, ours got lost, and we almost missed each other.

We stumbled along life and passed one another through the years until finally, like a beautiful mountain view, it was too difficult for us to walk away.

It could have been a romantic scene when we shook hands across a kitchen table. But it wasn't for us—not yet anyway. Our eyes did not lock. Fireworks did not ignite above us and drip slowly to the ground. Their colors would have to wait. We hardly noticed one another. Instead, we were consumed with the bustle of party favors, rehearsals and baby's breath. There was work to be done for the wedding, after all.

Every young woman and man wants to push past the playing and into the committed forever. We all want to become the knot tied that can never be undone, the water poured that can never be regained and the dance only two can perform.

But I was sixteen and a delicate new bud on a growing tree stretching up and out. Marriage was the last thing on my mind, and weddings were a bore. I was desperate for my tomboy image, which followed me throughout childhood. Caught in the middle of a maturing girl and an even younger woman, I remained a mystery, especially to myself. Sure, romance *would* come, but I prayed it would come slowly like the oceans inching their way up in the tides. No. I wanted it even slower than that. The makings of a huge maple—a bad habit working to change. But each day, my jeans got shorter, and my shoes got tighter. Deodorant and make-up started working hard to hide what was quickly becoming a reality: I was growing up.

Others noticed. I was a young yearling, wide-eyed and scared to death as I wound my way through the auction bid. Numbers flashed as potential buyers looked me over. A few started bidding for my affections, but it was never right. So I continued on, pretending I didn't care.

And then, my brother and his sister were getting married. Six years my senior and completely in love, Matt, my brother, had stolen her heart. She became 'his one.' Her gentle spirit and kind mid-western heart won the entire family. His luck was unbelievable. Some of us contemplated confronting her and reminding her that she could do better. But we realized they were perfect for one another; like scales on a fish lain out just right.

The engagement followed with pictures of a shiny diamond and slap-happy smiles. A spring wedding was scheduled and scribbled in. We all waited for the day. She would share it with her closest friend, her sister, and I would be attending my first double wedding.

We packed and studied the map. My parents, the groom, my younger sister and myself loaded up. We were on our way to Indiana—somewhere I had never been. The trip seemed endless. The car shrunk with each passing mile as my brother drove me close to madness with his good fortune. I was thankful he wouldn't be traveling home with us and prayed desperately the bride had not changed her mind. I began missing home, ignoring the excitement and trying instead to become consumed with one of my grandmother's innocent Christian romance novels.

The city arrived and with it the winds and rain. It blew and drove icy waters into every nook and cranny of our bodies. I missed our mountains. They knew how to block menacing winds like this—the kind that go right through to your bones. I shivered in my short-sleeved dress, goose bumps covering my arms. My toes hung over my now-too-small sandals, and I sighed in defeat. I leaned against a wall watching a stressed photographer attempt to capture the day inside his camera. Two brides at once was an almost impossible task. They smiled and posed, veils and skirts pestered, teased and fluffed into position after position after position. It was going to be a long day.

Somewhere in the frenzy of wet and wind, I saw him. He was quiet. Preparing for his sister's big day, he confidently did as he was told. He set up, he took down and he lugged chairs back and forth. He smiled for the pictures and then moved easily around the church. I watched from a distance—his tux just a bit big for his body.

His father was there. He would soon be losing his two daughters, and if that weren't enough, he would be the one carrying out the deed. Marrying them himself, his pastoral calling easily stretched to its max. The loss had to be bittersweet, unlike another loss he experienced many years before.

Gary's life was once much different. He was well established and rich, not only in worldly ways but in the deepest kinds. Four young kids and a lovely wife graced his life. He was blessed. Life was normal. Training wheels, gymnastics, baseballs and bats kept the young family busy. And like most, they were simply living, minding themselves and instilling God's truths into little hearts.

The tragedy came too quickly. Goodbyes never said. The children, the youngest five, the eldest twelve, were left motherless. A husband was left without his best friend, his wife, his lover. The speeding car came too fast for Gary to do anything but watch it unfold, the impact intense. The drunk killed her instantly and took another as well—a young man just trying to make his way home.

Gary was found on the trunk of his car. Legs twisted and caught in his seat belt with bones broken. He stared at the sky, his wife of fifteen years dead. Above him in the blackness of night, stars twinkled and winked. They were witnessing a new soul entering Heaven's gates. She was a special one. Perhaps that was why she had to go.

There were so many at the funeral, yet the most important was missing. Gary couldn't attend. His pelvis was shattered, and they told him he'd never walk. The children left in the arms of family members were forced to say goodbye to someone they weren't ready to let go. Life was once simple—the hardest part choosing a particular ice cream, a dress, or shoes. Turmoil, fear and sadness now resided. They were all forced to grow up too quickly. Gone were the tender kisses, the hugs and the love only a mother can give. Graham kicked at the casket, desperate to get to her. He was too young, just five.

Gary walked again, the pins and metal holding him together physically while love and support from family, friends and his Savior held him together in every other way. Life attempted to go back to normal. It was a new normal, uncomfortable and un-wanted. But they had no choice. The clock of life continued to tick on for them all. It was slow, painful.

The drunk was jailed and served four years for killing two lives. He heard the simple truth of God's love for him, his need for Him. Gary made sure of that. And just like Jesus forgave the guilty, the young widower with children also forgave.

In time, joy returned. Laughter floated once again through Saturday morning bedrooms and shoulders stretched out like new butterfly wings.

Then she came like the morning's bright sunny rays streaming through a dark room. Her life was just what he needed. Gary's heart felt love once again.

Some thought taking on this crew was crazy but not Kathy. To her, they were worth saving. A young thirty with no children of her own, she prepared mentally for the task at hand. They married quickly, and the honeymoon was even quicker. Noth-ing could've prepared her for what was ahead. Rough was an understatement. Attitudes and back-talking coupled with a new and inexperienced mother spelled disaster. The children had run loose far too long, and her attempts at reining them in were like salt on open wounds. Cuts dug deep with relationships taking years to mend.

Walls quickly went up. Parts of the heart, once tender, locked themselves away. They were thrown into the deepest depths, hardening on the way down. The hurt was too much to deal with. Like water wearing away at a jagged rock or stone, time became a type of salve, smoothing and healing. Smoothing and healing. Rubbing and rubbing and rubbing. It rubbed away the old and began forming something new. Slowly, a different stone emerged forcing the water of their lives to find a new way.

And that day, two daughters were getting married. I sat up front, watching my brother prepare himself. The professed love and proclaimed vows. I wondered if I would ever get to experience this for myself. All the things you think you should do before you die: careers, love, marriage, kids, growing old. I had my doubts about the possibility but held on to hope.

The boy, the young man in front who would someday be mine, cried the hardest that day. He was completely foreign to me. I didn't think he'd be losing anything today too. He was, though. I watched him, his tender heart spread out for everyone to see. A reddened face and streaming tears were hard to hide behind. He didn't care who saw. He had no one to impress, but he impressed me.

That was the first time I truly noticed him. I saw his sweet spirit, his quiet ways. He didn't even know it, but he raised his bid card, placing an offer on my heart. Rain pelted the roof of the church, but inside the sun shone bright and clear, the storm clouds easily forgotten.

My insignificant encounters with Graham were left behind right along with Indiana. I continued through a high school filled with sports, friends and school plays, unaware that he would be the one to finally release my foggy head of its prison, shaking it free. Our next meeting would not be forgotten.

A vacation to our woods with his entire family proved what he knew about himself already. He wanted this life, the kind with the mountains, and he wanted me.

I whistled for our horses, their reply a raise of two heads. Not until I jiggled the can of grain did they move their hooves in our direction. My sister and I stood waiting, our foreheads sweating in the summer heat. Renee reached for one as I clipped another, and we were off for the saddles. I heard in the distance the car pulling up the drive. They were here.

Graham, his older brother and the entire family spilled from the car with cameras in hand and smiles plastered on expectant faces. It was quite clear they had never experienced a life like this. Bags held a lifetime supply of sun block and bug spray. Their shoes were far too clean as they trudged toward us. Renee and I smiled at each other and continued brushing the horses.

My new sister-in-law, Abby, led the way. She was eager to show her family the life she married into. Her oversized camera clicked a continuous stream of pictures. Posing and touching the horses with caution, the pictures would give the essence of experience; they would look great in the scrapbook, but they showed a tall tale. Nervous smiles told of the fear underneath the surface, but the fear wasn't enough to stop them. They were still willing to ride.

"You're not going to be able to ride in that." My eyes scanned Graham but moved to Abby.

"What's wrong with what I'm wearing?" His voice was genuine, inexperience evident.

City Boys.

I leaned against the horse, the saddle secure and ready for the mount. I caught Renee's eye. She tried not to smile.

43

"You're going to chafe if you wear those shorts."

Their eyes dropped to their cargo shorts and skater shoes. It was pathetic. Tee shirts marked with symbols I didn't understand clung tightly to their hosts. The shorts were worn loose, and they looked like they were about to fall. Fortunately, a belt held them in place. It didn't look like their shoes were even tied. Apparently, they were in style.

"It'll be okay for today." I bridled the horses in one easy motion, certain they didn't even realize it.

"We won't go far," Renee added.

Their smiles returned. They were ready for a basic lesson. I found myself partnered with the older brother. Rick was eager to try anything once and listened carefully to my advice. I noticed how his red hair matched his father's perfectly. He was naturally athletic and broad shouldered. He climbed easily onto my horse and grabbed at the reins. I scurried up next, sitting easily behind the saddle. Relaxed a bit when I gripped the cantle, he kissed to the horse as I told him to, and we were soon heading down a familiar trail, a safe one.

Renee worked carefully with Graham, eagerness and excitement written all over his face. He was taking it seriously, soaking up every bit of help, trying desperately to be the rider he pictured in his head. He stayed calm and moved easily with his horse. Even with his hair buzzed short, I could still make out the brown color. He resembled his brother in almost every way except the hair. He was somewhat shorter too. They were both about my height. I was beginning to accept my lanky legs, long torso and arms. I would never be the small girl with petite feet and hands I so desperately wanted.

Graham made up for his lack of height in brute strength. His legs were thick, almost too muscled. He was stocky for his age without an ounce of fat on him. I was certain no one had ever picked a fight with him. He was even more athletic than his older brother, his balance and movements evident even on a horse. He claimed he played baseball, a pitcher. I had a hard time seeing it. He looked more like a wrestler to me.

The riders had much to learn and did the basic things people do when on a horse for the first time. Their legs tensed and held the sides of the horse as if that would save them. Their seats bounced with each step, quickly making it painful for them and the horses. A white-knuckled hand clung to the horn while the other held the reins too high.

It was awkward.

I was thankful our horses were forgiving and patient.

Thinking they were ready for something more daring, they asked to trot. It didn't last long. Cries of pain and discomfort forced us to walk once again. Renee and I laughed and poked fun at the city boys.

Even with the easy ride the horses sweated in the intense heat. We unsaddled, and Graham climbed up onto my horse, Maverick. He sat behind me as we headed into the cool waters bareback. Like a carousel ride, the horses dipped up and down before smoothing out and swimming with ease. They snorted and groaned with pleasure. The water was perfect, and the horses stood while we took turns jumping off their backs.

The boys liked the country life, especially Graham. He had been a caged animal, forced into a place he didn't want to call home. Here though, he belonged—fit for the first time. This was home.

Their time with us flew by. We played, talked and laughed together that week. We went on several more rides; Graham's abilities grew and advanced each time. He was a natural rider. What he would become as a horseman started here. He took off quickly and his abilities would soon surpass my own and everyone else around.

When they left, I felt sick. Like a dog left behind while their human friend goes away, it just didn't feel right. But I had no choice. We said our goodbyes, never hinting or knowing what the other truly felt. We had only sixteen years on us with 800 miles in between. I was certain it would never work.

5
A RAINY DAY YES

'Twenty years from now you will be more disappointed by the things that you didn't do than by the ones you did do. So throw off the bowlines. Sail away from the safe harbor. Catch the trade winds in your sails. Explore. Dream. Discover.'
~ H. Jackson Brown Jr.

Hundreds had witnessed them fall. And by now news had spread like wildfire. A fast 48 hours and thousands knew—many from other countries and even more from all over the States. I had to give updates. They were waiting. They were wondering. His condition was critical.

Everyday I grabbed my computer and sat quietly next to his bed typing. The clicks from my fingers harmonized perfectly with the life-giving machines. Writing became an outlet, a way to deal.

At times, I felt I was writing about someone else. A character in a play. An actor. Someone dealt a bad hand in life. This couldn't be happening to *me*. But it was. And the plot thickened at each turn, the relief in writing only temporary.

Like those carried to and fro in litters, the shoulders of slaves burning and cramping with fatigue, I was lifted. Those endless pleas for Graham's life to be spared got me through the darkest of days. They carried me. I felt them continuously—even at night when sleep abandoned me. I needed prayer just like eyes need to blink. Graham needed them even more.

It didn't take long for the story to unfold, to shape and to mold itself. It turned into its own kind of life with feelings and breath. Now if only Graham would do the same without all the help.

His family came. His dad. His mom. His brother and sisters. We all believed he'd awaken in hours—a few days at the most. They all wanted to be here for it when it happened.

I dreamed it like a movie. A moan here. A finger twitch there. A slow eye blink to open followed by tears of joy. Laughter spilling into the hallways as we would hug, cling to each other, thank God for life. Graham's life. The disruption a mere blip in the radar.

It became clear within a few days that my thoughts of his waking up would not come to pass as I imagined. It became evident his family wasn't only here for him. But me. They were here if he didn't make it, here if I had to make those harsh decisions.

Graham couldn't hold me, cry with me or feel anything for that matter. But his family could. And they were the closest thing to him I could get. That red-haired brother of his, the one Graham grew up with, played with, was bittersweet to be around. Rick stood by his side, trying to talk, trying to laugh, trying to be strong. He wasn't fooling me.

I had never seen him cry, yet there he stood, tears streaming down his face, unashamed as he tried to stick small white earphones into Graham's ears from his Ipod. We were told it could help.

Several days in and the doctors placed an inter-cranial pressure valve into Graham's brain. It was a long metal contraption, which protruded from his now partially shaved head. The whole scene reminded me of some sort of robotic unicorn. Various wires and equipment spilled from it, providing information. There were red ones, blue ones, green ones and white. To me it seemed like a botched job with all the medical tape and plastic linings surrounding it. But this piece, although odd looking and perhaps a bit messy, provided a wealth of knowledge about Graham.

It measured the pressure inside and gave it a number, an ICP number. It flashed green, a black screen behind it, traveling from one end to another before disappearing completely. It was simple really. A high number meant high pressure, with the brain swelling and having no place to go, it could kill him. The doctors removing a section of his skull was highly possible.

No one in his room could take their eyes off it. Beeping and beeping like the snooze on my alarm clock, it was pushed again and again. We were desperate for silence. But his brain continued to swell and the beeps continued as the long days ticked away.

Each day I'd make my way to the hospital elevators. Having learned quickly that staying in Graham's room the whole night was torture, I slept in my uncle's motor home most nights.

The room was too lonely. The noises, the stillness, the darkness. At first, when I tried to stay, I could almost feel my fingernails being ripped from their digits with a pair of rusty pliers. Maybe I was too weak, or selfish, or scared to be alone. Whatever the reason, I couldn't be there.

Every day, I stepped in, my hand reaching out to press the bright circular number staring back at me. I needed number 3. The third level. The floor Graham was on. What I really wanted was to press number 6—the snuggery floor with all those new-born babies where parent's cooed and awed over new life, where everything was well in the world. I pumped myself up, praying, pleading for strength. Somehow, I was able to push it, the doors sliding shut, locking me in. My destiny set.

It dinged up. It wouldn't be a long ride. I leaned against the back wall, trying to enjoy the music. But I didn't usually listen to this stuff. I didn't usually ride in elevators. And I surely didn't enjoy hanging out on the ICU floor. I was completely out of my comfort zone. Faster than I was ready, the doors opened. I was forced to step out.

It's a depressing place—the dreaded ICU.

Like the new kid at a big school, I adjusted. It wasn't fun. Many days had now equipped me for what I encountered. But my stomach still sank when I saw them.

A large group of people stood quietly in one of the many waiting rooms, or holding cells, as I now called them. Their faces said it all. Loss. Fear. Confusion. Questions. Tears. They huddled and cried, waiting just as I had for answers. I tried to pass on tip-toes, my flip-flops hanging from my heels. It wouldn't have mattered if I marched by playing a tuba though. I wasn't noticed. Shock was thick. And everywhere.

I reached for the main phone, big, locked double doors waited in front of me, and the only way in was through this phone. I lifted it from its cradle and pressed it to my ear. It was cool.

"Nurse's station, how can I help you?" She was friendly.

"I'm here to see Graham Stump, Room D329. This is his wife." I put on a strong voice, hoping I would sound convincing. Like tears weren't right at the surface.

"One moment please."

Silence while she went to check with his nurse.

I coiled the cord around my fingers then squirted a huge glob of hand sanitizer on my palms. There was enough to go up my arms to my elbows. So I did.

"Come right in." A buzz followed, unlocking the doors.

Afraid I'd missed my opportunity I bolted toward them like a racehorse bolts out of its starting gate. I dropped the phone in its place. Perhaps a bit rough.

There were no cheers, no admiring screams like the racehorses get as they wind their way around the track to the finish line.

Complete silence. The doors swung closed behind me, followed by a click. I was in. My eyes searched the scene.

Medical staff scurried here and there, busily completing their tasks with care. Portable machines on wheels sat in just about every open space—some waiting to be used, others being pushed and pulled to a new place. A new patient. The first few feet of wall on either side covered itself thick with thank you cards and pictures hung with tape, tacks, glue; many smiled back at me.

The photos held family and that loved one, who almost didn't make it, clinging joyfully to staff and nurses. A note, carefully written in thanksgiving. That one had been healed. It was a small piece of hope for me.

So many people. Staff and patient alike. So eerily quiet. Like the local library, only worse. Much worse. Instead of the flipping pages of one engrossed or studying for an exam, it was the quiet beeps of countless machines, keeping someone alive. A phone ringing softly in the distance. The swish-swish of nurse's scrubs walking back and forth, sometimes fast, sometimes slow. Each beep needing attention, they continued to sing their tune of distress like hungry babies.

The trauma ICU floor. A rough place to be. It had victims from car accidents, falls, ATV accidents. All the beds appeared full. At times curtains were drawn while someone was changed, bathed or worked on. But most of the time, the curtains were open. And I could peer right in. Machines just like Graham's worked hard to breathe, feed and medicate those they were hooked in. Their bodies so still. Too still.

Some sat up in bed but not by choice. Bed sores a real issue, they had to be moved and rotated every few hours. Pillows were propped and fluffed and placed carefully for support. Many patients slept on, their nurses wiping and checking. Adjusting and fixing, trying desperately to nurse them back. It was this way for Graham. And I was in the same boat as those around me, watching the clock, the machines.

Others were conscious. Aware. And totally unable to do anything about it. Their two beady eyes the only thing moving. Searching, seeking. Trying to communicate.

I slipped into his room and also a kiss to his forehead. He smelled different today. Like plastic and hospital and medicines I didn't recognize. I missed *his* smell. The one with water and woods and horse mixed in with that hard-earned sweat from work. He was ashen and clammy and what hair was left needed a good washing. I decided instead to have them shave it all off.

His nurse, quiet and professional, pushed that beeping button again and again. It was the one for the pressure. I cringed as I watched the numbers climb.

Several tense moments passed.

"It's very important to stay calm and quiet while you're here." She adjusted his neck brace since having calmed the monitor, the numbers slowly descending back to normal.

"Do you think he knows I'm here?" Hopeful, I reached for his fingers. Still rough. Still calloused. A bit of dark stain lining his prints, deep in those cracks that he never could seem to get clean no matter how long he scrubbed at them.

"He may. With his numbers climbing like that, he could have sensed something. But, he won't remember it." She dabbed his face, moved some of his blankets. And turned to go.

I reached for the chair in the corner of his room. I drug it across the tiles closer to his bed with a loud moan. It didn't want to go. Slumping down, its hard seat and stiff armrests created an unwelcoming break for my bones.

Graham didn't notice my discomfort. How could he? He was in a coma. I wanted to scream at him. See if that would make a difference. See if it would help. I looked outside his room and contemplated it. No one was around. Maybe they wouldn't know it was me. Maybe I could get away with it. All I wanted was for him to open his eyes. To remember me. To tell me it was going to be okay. I swallowed it down as a young girl pushed a bucket of soapy water down the halls.

My eyes burned. Hot tears rolling down, my vision blurry. My throat got that swelling feeling, like a bad allergy reaction, making it hard to breathe.

He had said it before. That it would all be okay, that we had nothing to worry about. That God had a plan for us. A plan involving him. He just didn't know what it was.

This couldn't be it. Could it?

I wanted to talk to him more than anything in that moment. Ask him if this was what he signed up for that day in the rain.

"Remember the tree I cut up in the yard, the one from the storm?" My mind replayed his question to me.

"Of course I do." The pine was thick, dense, the trunk massive. I never understood why it fell. Of all the smaller trees around it, the storm took this one down as well as our power. Graham spent the next day cutting, chopping, stacking—the rain only a light mist now. I watched from the kitchen window, the chainsaw smoking and spewing bits of creamy powder onto his boots, his pants. Feet balanced effortlessly on the horizontal tree, arms moving back and forth slicing branches and limbs.

"The Lord talked to me out there. Clear as day." His eyes searched mine, scanning back and forth, waiting for that sinking reaction.

"Really?" I was doubtful. And maybe a bit jealous.

"What'd He say?" I had to ask.

"He asked me if I'd be willing." The edges of his fingers grasped our counter. He was bracing himself for the words about to escape my mouth. Like they would hit him full force, knock him over. He was probably smart to hold tight.

"And?"

"That was it. That was all He asked. But, I told him, 'Yes.'"

"I want to be willing to do more for Him, Randi. Whatever He has for me, for us. I want to do it."

I wasn't sure I liked where the conversation was going. I sank onto the stool near our island. My hand rested on my growing belly and as if on cue, Keith jumped inside me.

"You have no idea what He could want you to do?"

"No."

"Will we have to move?"

"Maybe." He shrugged his shoulders.

"You have no education Graham. No training." My practicality was setting in deep. And I was just getting warmed up.

"I know."

We're having another baby. We just finished this house. I thought he was happy here. I wanted to say it. Yell it actually. How could he do this to me? This unsettling feeling knocked at my heart's door, begging to set up camp.

"We don't have to make any decisions yet. Just pray." He reached for me.

I knew I felt stiff in his arms. But I didn't care.

"Will you do something for me?"

I nodded my head against his chest, using his own body as a shield to hide my concern, fear. I didn't want him to see.

"Will you pray about this with me? Just pray. That's all I'm asking."

I suppose I could pray. It doesn't mean we have to make a decision yet. Leave our jobs. Sell the house. Move the family. I could be worrying over nothing. What harm could prayer bring? In a few weeks, it'll blow over anyway. He'll have forgotten. The fire in him will have died.

"Okay, I'll pray."

My answer satisfied him.

"It's going to be okay. Everything will work out. He loves us, Randi. Look at the blessings He's given us." He was talking into my neck, still holding me.

I wanted to believe him. I truly did. And I wanted his faith. His devotion. His unwavering trust in Someone he couldn't see. Or touch.

Graham had heard Him. And he had been willing.

Willing even for this? I wasn't so sure.

His enthusiasm for God's plan got him a front row bed in the ICU. Tubes everywhere. His dignity stripped. His modesty taken. Future unknown.

Is this what you had in mind all along God? Was this your big question to Graham that day in the rain? To see if he'd be willing to lie here in a coma with this head injury surviving on life support?

My teeth gritted like an angry child. A spoiled child. This wasn't what I wanted. Graham may have signed up for this. But I never did. I felt trapped. Unsure. Hurt.

Hurt by Him. Jesus. The One supposed to be my Protector.

I still loved Him. But I was having a really hard time trusting Him with my husband's life, my kids' lives, His ability to really heal Graham. That He truly had everything under control. And that it was all for my good.

Staring at his hospital gown, a most ugly dress-like drape, like a sack, unflattering and unattractive, I knew. My whole being knew.

This was exactly what the Lord meant with His question that day. He had it in mind all along. Even back then. Almost two years before.

And there we were. No plans. No agenda. And absolutely no control.

6
SANDPIT SUICIDE

'Character cannot be developed in ease and quiet. Only through experience of trial and suffering can the soul be strengthened, vision cleared, ambition inspired, and success achieved.'
~Helen Keller

I wasn't so awkward anymore. I had grown into my legs. A torso once too long was more fitting, more becoming. My hair had thickened, and it now mattered how the strands fell across my shoulders; I burned my neck trying to curl the locks but soon mastered the art. I even dabbled in the aisles picking and sorting through mascara, eyeliner and shadows to dress my lids, liking the browns and grays. I started caring not for any reason other than it was time.

I knew who I was, not in arrogance, but rather recognition, acceptance. Past loves had taught me not only to guard *my* heart but theirs as well. I was done with the game. I was content to wait.

A year of Bible school helped. I learned and fastened myself in a richer way to my faith and love for Christ. I soaked up what I could and kept my eyes on the end goal determined to finish strong. Like the tortoise in his big race against the hare it would be slow and steady for me. But I'd do it.

News reached me of a possible return. His return. I was eighteen, he the same. I tried not to care. He was coming to paint houses, not play with me. I heard his reasons and continued my act of nonchalance. In his free time, he wanted to fly-fish. He wanted to hike. He wanted to breathe our air and spread the wings that had been held down far too long. But honestly, I hoped for deeper reasons—reasons that involved me.

I was nervous as to what he had become through the years. What would I find in him? Even worse, what would he find in me? I cautiously waited. I had to swallow hard when my heart threatened to beat out of my throat.

Graham, in fact, had changed a great deal even more than I. His face no longer held signs of the boy I first saw. Sharp features had chiseled themselves deep into the man he was becoming. He remained a mystery, confident and sure—one I wanted to solve.

There was something else too. I could sense but couldn't quite grasp it completely. His sea glass eyes were deeper. Like a once shallow beach carved out by fierce waves, the ones that foam and crash big, something had changed him. Someone had happened to him. I observed and watched him once again—just like at the wedding a few years before.

An Indian summer day, hot with the sun sitting low in the sky would be the start for us. Mayflies and other bugs danced close to the ground searching and floating about, the sun's rays revealing the multitude. The grass was dry and stiff. You could feel her thirst for water with each step to the barn. It crunched. It cried.

Work done for the day, Graham asked to ride. He wanted to continue his education. He came with jeans this time, blue and fitted. He still had those skater shoes; it looked as if he'd walk right out of them at any moment. To my surprise, he never did. He helped me brush, tack, bridle. Smells of paint and pine lingered on him. A pink spot above his left eyebrow gave me a small hint of what his day had been like. Rather than give off the soft and feminine appearance the color was known for, it somehow made him more rugged.

He mounted Maverick once again with a little more ease than he had years before. A brown stripe started at the horse's withers and worked its way to the base of his tail. When I was little, I thought zebra ran through his blood.

Maverick was a good horse, simple, patient and well mannered. He had taught me much through the years like how to perfect my bareback skills and basic trick riding. I'd stand on his back, my bare feet dirty from the pasture, and we would trot all over the place. My sister and I got quite good at it. We wanted to be circus performers. We were certain there would be a place for us in their show.

Maverick and I were the same age, born only months apart. Trained by my parents they poured over books and magazines learning the ways of horse training and psychology. For never having done it before, they did a fine job. He moved through my brother's hands and eventually into mine. As a child, I occasionally found myself flying through the air, catching glimpses of his face on my way to the ground. I knew he was laughing at me, testing me and pushing me to be ready for that next time, the next take off or flight back to the barn. It was all from my inexperience. But by now we had finally reached an agreement. That trust and bond had formed. We were old friends that barrel raced and worked our way through the many trails and streams surrounding the house.

"Feel ok?" I reached for Graham's stirrups to adjust them. I automatically grabbed at his calf and moved it forward to rest just in front of the fender. He waited as I moved and fiddled with the blevins buckle. I finally got it right.

"Okay, Cowboy, I think you're set." His feet now easily reached the stirrups. I hoped he hadn't noticed how much shorter I had to make them. Those stirrups had been set for my legs. I moved them back into the correct position and tried to force his heels down. I explained the proper equitation seat—how the shoulders should look, the back, legs, hands. He appeared to be listening, to be taking it all in once again. But, I wasn't sure. He was making me feel uneasy, nervous. It was how he looked at me. Like he saw right through that plastic wrap covering into the Tupperware container full of spoiled, smelly leftovers. I had trouble making eye contact, afraid to give him a chance.

We started out just the two of us down trails and paths I had run on countless times as a young girl. The horses walked lazily in the heat; we barely noticed, too lost in conversation. While Graham was learning a better seat he was also trying to learn me. I wondered which one he was having a harder time with.

Our ride took us near one of my favorite places. It was odd, this place I liked. Perhaps that was why. We turned the horses up that way. To her.

There she sat—a big lot of land once beautiful. But I never saw her like that. Her glory days long over, the odds and ends were all that remained. No trees, no grass, not even much wildlife. Just a dug out hole in the middle of some hills, stripped bare.

Some rocks spaced themselves throughout what was left. And that was it.

She had been the town sandpit, supplying the sand for our icy roads for years, no one ever giving thought to the security she provided. Pieces of her sprinkled our entire town, pulling and tending the vehicles, the drivers. She had been taken advantage of, raped and left with horrible scars. Now, there was nothing to make her beautiful again. Nothing left for anyone to want. Oh, they tried to make her presentable, but the damage had already been done, the walls too high for anything to grow. She was sold for almost nothing. Wasted.

I went to her all the time as a child sliding on her steep hills, filling my shoes and pants with sand. I sat on her rocks and watched the clouds float overhead. For some reason, she made everything more open, more easily seen, at least to me. I wandered and crawled to the edge where the berries grew. It was the only thing that did. I ate my fill and even brought some home, my shirt stained purple. My mom made pies and jam from her bounty.

Graham and I stood together on one of her edges looking down deep inside. The horses' hooves beat out a rhythm attempting to shoo the menacing flies. There was a trail going to the bottom, but Graham wanted to see the hills and watch the crows glide over top us. The small breeze from up here filled our lungs. It was clear, fresh.

"Do you see that car?" Graham pointed with his hand, my eyes moving in the same direction.

A white car sat parked some distance away from us. It was impossible to see anyone. It was just a small speck from where we were. But unless someone knew this pit, they would never come. Who would want to visit a place so abandoned as this?

A few of the locals would make the turn up the sandy drive sometimes to drink, shoot their guns and do some 'neckin', as my grandfather would often say.

"What do you think they're doing down there?" I was certain it was the latter, the 'neckin' part.

I looked at Graham who in turn looked back and smiled.

"Let's sneak up and scare 'em."

"They're probably just a couple of teenagers down there making out," he continued, his hands grabbing the reins to turn Maverick around. But, the horse was acting strange. Something was amiss.

"Keep him moving." I encouraged. Most likely a deer was bounding just ahead of us. A large white tail raised in alarm. But I saw nothing. Heard nothing. Later, his antics would make sense.

We wound along the backside of the pit, hiding easily behind the walls and tree line. Soon we turned onto a road forcing us to face the car head on. We whispered quietly, not wanting to ruin the plan.

The car was not from here. That was easily noted as the license plate came into better view.

Arizona plates. A white Ford Mustang with the silver running pony emblem blared back at me. Kind of ironic, I thought, as the horses plodded along. No thoughts of running on their minds.

I pressed on leading the way. Hooves clipped along easily. It was the only sound around. That was strange. Even the crows overhead had grown quiet. Graham tagged behind, trying his best to get Maverick to come to life. He was always kind of lazy.

This will be fun. I smiled and prepared myself for the laugh building in my stomach. It was the kind I did when nervous, excited or otherwise when I should've been serious.

I began to make out a form, a body or two, moving slightly. My grandpa was right. People really did come here for 'neckin'. I looked back at Graham, my smile huge.

Something had changed in Graham's face. A silent warning.

"Be careful, Randi." His voice was different. Nervous.

My eyes rolled. And I began to realize his city instincts were kicking in. He had much to learn about the mountains and Schroon Lake. I gave him a respectful nod pretending I agreed. He'd soon learn nothing happened here. Our town was the quiet, forgotten kid in the corner. And we liked it that way. We felt safe being forgotten. No trouble came here.

We still had excitement, of course, but not like the city. Not like where Graham came from. We didn't have to worry about the robberies, the shootings, the attacks.

Ours came from moose sightings, stuck snowmobiles, blizzards, days of power outages from storms, or from parked cars with whom the participants inside skirted around each other.

I decided to head for the driver's side window. That side carried all the action. I looked closer, my eyes straining a bit to focus. There weren't two people in there. Just one, a big one, moving slightly as if in sleep.

It was a man, his head tilted back on the headrest. He had to be sleeping. Eyes closed and mouth a bit open. My thoughts circled around his sleep, his possible dreams, snoring.

He must have pulled off here to get some rest. Arizona is a long drive.

By now I was almost to him, ready to carry out the big surprise. He continued moving, jerking and thrashing a bit. Something inside me told me it wasn't right. But there I sat atop the horse, right above him, looking down through the clear window. I peered back at Graham, my puzzled face saying everything to him.

"There's blood coming out of his ear." It was a confused response.

He convulsed, and I jumped from the horse. I had to help. My hand reached for the doorknob white, clean.

"Randi, don't do it!" Graham came close, still sitting on Maverick.

"But, he's hurt. We have to do something." I turned once again, just inches from him.

"Leave him! We don't know what's he capable of."

"Ride back with me for help." Seconds ticked on as I debated with myself. I looked to Graham and back at the man struggling for air. He was bigger than me, and maybe *he* was the one playing the prank all along.

"Let's get help." Graham tried again, eyes pleading with me. He was genuinely concerned for me. For us.

I selfishly thought nothing of Graham as I mounted quickly and sped home. I knew Maverick would make it. But, I wasn't so sure he'd still have his rider, but I never looked back.

I didn't have to steer. My sister's horse knew the way. And I let her take me up the road, the white house quickly coming into view.

We made it in one piece, though Graham's hair was a bit disheveled and a short, red scratch was now on his cheek. He touched it with his hand and smiled. That low branch must have gotten him. But his bottom had stayed in the saddle. And his smile said it all. He was going to want to do that again.

We didn't even untack the horses, just left them in the yard grazing my father's perfect lawn. We called 911. The police were soon on their way.

We raced back on foot this time, the distance not far. I needed to know. I wanted to see for myself what I knew would most likely unfold.

It was as we suspected. He was still. Too still. The massive chest no longer fought for breath. The convulsions stopped. Ten minutes had been too long to be gone. My heart ached for him.

What was his story?

I stood peering through the window once again. Graham wouldn't let me touch anything, but I was still curious. I had to find answers. Blood had dripped from his left ear and trickled down his neck to his shoulder. It was already starting to dry. Stubble from a day's worth of growth looked like pepper on his face. His button-up shirt was stained in blood. Oversized hands rested to the side of the seat, draped and motionless.

I scanned the back seat and saw newspapers scattered about, opened as if they had been searched and pilfered through. There was a box of doughnuts, some more papers. But, otherwise the car was clean, much cleaner than the rust bucket I drove around. That Dodge Ram Charger was clunky, rusty and nothing like this beautiful white Mustang. I was lucky if the Dodge would start for me, even luckier when no pieces fell onto the road, forcing me to turn around and pick up a muffler or fender. I needed to vacuum it. Animals would soon be making their home in it and I'd eventually smell the residuals of their presence.

"Well, that's what happened to him," Graham announced, his eyes looking intently, his finger pointing but avoiding contact with the glass. My mind came back to reality.

"What do you see?" I moved to get a closer look, and that's when I saw it.

The handgun rested peacefully between his seat and center consol. A black 9mm stared precariously back at us. It sat stunned in the darkness as if afraid to come out from its hiding place. Graham had been looking for it all along. And now, like a fog lifting from the lake, I saw everything clearly. I could see across to the other side. And it all made sense.

That moment of fear Maverick experienced was when the gun must have exploded. He was the only one who heard, the only one who knew something wasn't right.

Graham and I stared at it for a moment longer. Our eyes eventually reached each other. They were huge. We were thinking the same thing.

"If we had been just a few minutes earlier...." Graham couldn't finish. But I did.

"Who knows what he would have done to us."

We sat near the car, waiting for the police. There was nothing more we could do.

It wouldn't take long. The locked car was broken into. He was removed with those grunting and sweating to get the job done. A body bag zipped up and over his large frame. The stretcher carried him to the waiting ambulance. There was no rush, no need to hurry.

Police had their questions. Pads with pens scribbled our answers. I almost cowered when their eyes peered out from just underneath their hats. I had nothing to hide yet felt like hiding.

Intimidation was their friend. We signed on the dotted line and were ripped a copy or two for safekeeping. A few thanked us for our efforts and quick response. They soon all pulled away, the dust rising softly around us. The pit grew quiet once again. The crows came back, cawing and flying circles above our heads. No other noise reached our ears. The storm had passed. The only thing that still remained was that mustang. Its windows pierced and shattered, small shards glittering the ground.

We eventually wandered back along the path we had raced earlier in the day. But I didn't want to go home yet. Neither did he.

We walked to the river below our road. Large rocks placed themselves perfectly in a line forcing a waterfall to flirt and jive across. Springtime was when we'd venture the rapids, shooting over them on those small black inner tubes. My dad always led the way. They were just big enough for a quick rush of adrenaline followed by laughter and shivering bodies.

Summer brought the more peaceful, warm, and shallow falls. The suckers had long run their flight up river. They'd get stuck here at the falls, struggling and straining to get over them. Forming in a large group at the base they'd take turns jumping. Eventually they'd all make it. Growing up we'd catch them with our hands or use poles to snag them to shore. Only the leeches were left now with a few trout residing in the deep.

I found a place to sit. A smoothed out stone from the once rising waters worked perfectly. I tucked my knees to my chest in an effort to keep warm but didn't realize how late it was getting. The sun would be setting soon. Dragonflies flitted close by hunting for mosquitoes and bugs. Their drumming wings added to the water's song.

"You're different somehow. What's changed?" I couldn't wait any longer. I had to know.

Graham found a seat next to mine, his shoes digging into the stray stones, rolling them back and forth with his feet. His eyes scanned the foaming water for a moment before lifting to the sky. A few stars twinkled and fought for positions in their nightly debut.

Maybe he didn't hear me. The water was loud.

But his eyes made their way to mine. "I finally found Jesus."

My head tilted as questions bombarded my brain. But I fought the urge and stayed quiet.

"I know, shocking right?" He went on.

"A pastor's kid, growing up with all the right questions to ask and answers to give, missed it completely."

A slight breeze worked its way down the bend, forcing me to pull my hair from my eyes. I had to see him. I had to watch this. He was staring at the water again like it was about to reveal something grand, impressive.

"What happened to change it all for you?" I asked quietly, my eyes glued to his side profile.

"There were many, but the biggest actually, was meeting you."

I almost laughed out loud but caught it just in time. He couldn't have been more serious. I bit my cheek and waited, unsure what to say. My own eyes now awkwardly sought the water, desperate for that grand display.

"I've never met a girl like you. You're simple, easy to talk to, fun. Your love for the Lord. I want….." He stopped, suddenly aware he was saying these things out loud.

"You want what?" I had no idea what he would say.

There was no going back now.

"I want *you*. And I realized I'd have to make some pretty major changes in my life to get you, get a girl like you." He looked me straight on and continued.

"I've made some really bad decisions in my life. Really bad. But, after meeting you, I decided to start caring. I craved the Lord. I got saved, re-baptized and for the first time, my relationship with Jesus became alive, real."

The words flowed so easily from his mouth. His story. His journey. I sat still the whole time, watching his hands move with his words as if choreographed.

My mind spun. This was the difference in him. This was what had happened. Carefully and methodically, he laid his heart out. Not for me to inspect and sniff like a dog deciding on a meal, only to discard it for something better.

No.

His intentions clear, his motives genuine. There was only one thing for him to do.

"Can I see you?" His boldness was striking, attractive.

"Can I see just you?" He shifted to see me better. And waited like he had all the time in the world.

I could feel the heat lift to my face.

"I don't see any other guys lined up trying to bang down my door." I laughed nervously, trying to sound as smooth as he had. I was failing miserably.

He didn't seem to notice my awkwardness.

"You know I have to leave soon. And I don't know when I'll be back." He finally said it. We both knew it was right there under the surface. The reality of the distance soon forming between us was hard to think of. All that space. Eight hundred miles of it.

"We'll have to just take this thing a day at a time." I delivered him a wobbly smile. I said it more to myself than to him.

We'd never be ready for the day. Still, it came. Too quickly.

The car door soon slammed shut, his last bag filled with some shirts, pants, a toothbrush. He faithfully sported those now famous skater-shoes.

I didn't know it, but I'd never see those shoes again.

I hugged him tight, his scent still carrying the woods. I knew he'd come back to me. He promised he would.

But instead of those skater shoes with the untied laces and scuffed up sides, a pair of brown leather Ariat's would frame his feet.

7
THE BEACH START

'The happiest moments of my life have been the few which I have passed at home in the bosom of my family.'
~Thomas Jefferson

My world of work, kids, life, slowed like a well-executed half-halt, the kind where riders secretly hesitate the horse with hands and legs. I had always wanted more time. And suddenly, it was as abundant as ants on a piece of sticky candy. Sadly, I didn't want this kind of time. It hurt too much and left me reeling with thoughts of life, racking my brain. What did I do to deserve this? What had Graham done?

I just wanted to go back to normal.

But normal was gone—deleted—with the push of a backspace button, and there was no "Undo" option.

I allowed my thoughts to travel to happier times that could never be erased or changed.

And it started with them, the influence, their example in my life. Part of them was in me and would always be. I spun and twirled like a fancy top on the wooden floor for everyone to see. But, I was faltering. Losing ground and speed, the fall inevitable.

Even as I readied for the descent, I never doubted whose hands would be there to help pick me up.

They wouldn't be Graham's. He was in a coma, completely oblivious to his surroundings. No doubt they'd be the ones to set me spinning again.

They met at church. My mother's straight hair was striking and so long like the hippies. My father's was cut short, tamed and cultured. It was the way hers flew and swung that was too much for my dad—that and her bell-bottoms and her smile and all those things that shouldn't matter but do.

At 19, they toed the edge. Fingers laced. Eyes locked, they took the jump and never once looked back.

New Jersey could not corral their dreams of country living. The mountains were calling. A 40-acre lot was walked and purchased; a foundation dug and a small house plopped in the middle of it all. It was a start, a place to dream big without any limits on adventure.

And they had adventures.

They'd play and walk and ride the horses all over. They were first to discover the streams and the meadows surrounding their home. They blazed the trails I would one day run; the soft ground a cushion for my rough and calloused feet.

They hunted the woods and skied the lake. My mother always the driver as my father learned to bare foot. The hot pink wet suit complimented her blonde hair as she whipped the '69 Barracuda Correct Craft across the lake and back again.

When it was her turn, she would stand patiently where the water meets the sand, waiting for that beach start. Her right foot set in the wet black rubber, the other steadying next to it. You almost couldn't see the lone ski, mostly dark with a bit of green, hiding just inches under the water. We all learned on that ski.

A big loop formed from the rope gripping that and the handle in the same hands. The other end secured itself to the boat with my dad. Curly hair bounced the back of his neck like those old phone cords, the kind hardly seen these days. His hair was always long now, just about to his shoulder blades. The mountains had changed him for the better and so had she.

It was the nod, the way she flicked her head and shouted her readiness that always had us watching. I liked to sit in the seat next to Dad to help 'spot' her. I'd pull and yank my life jacket in place so I could get a good view. Just as the boat broke away, she'd throw the loop and skim the water, her free foot finding its home behind the other. She made it look so easy, like anyone could do it. And I only ever remember the tips of her hair getting wet. Never her whole head from falls or bad starts. When she tired of cutting back and forth across the wake she'd simply release the handle, sinking into the water. It'd swallow her slowly, like a snake eating too large a meal.

In a way they grew up together marrying young like that. But even in their youth they chose wisely. They wanted to use their home to raise the kids they talked about having. For them, it was the only way to do it.

And the kids came. Four of them.

Even the hardest of workers cannot truly describe my father. In his own quiet way without arrogance, he'd simply outwork the best. He was selfless. Blessed with the ability to fix anything, he found a calling as an auto-mechanic. Twelve years of crawling, scraping and sweating under the rust provided what we needed. But no more. We were poor, and I never knew it. They never let on.

His business did however produce a variety of vehicles to tool around in, the likes of which only ran because of his talents under the hood. A rusty hole in the floor, the size of a grapefruit allowed access for us to watch the sparkly pavement below. I liked watching the yellow lines best, especially the ones that dotted quickly by. Others we owned always had cracked windshields. And not just a small ding here or there from a pebble. These traveled up and across the entire shield, crisscrossing over and back again. It was more like a big spider web, and bugs slamming into the glass made it seem all the more real for me.

Working, for my dad, was not his life. Long hours meant food in our growing bellies, not something to define him. That kind of definition came from my mother. And from us. But mostly from the Lord. He marched to his own beat. The one pressing on his heart to instill, to teach, to love.

He welcomed fatherhood. Being a child in many ways himself, he taught us to play, to laugh, to work, but mostly to see Jesus in action. The mountains helped him. He'd pull a worn out map from his top dresser drawer and point to the hills and mountains surrounding our home. He knew all their names. We'd climb one, just any one we wanted, him leading the way, showing, telling stories, instructing us on so much more than the trees, rocks and wildlife living there. Our little eyes and hearts must have been listening. We all saw. We all took in the view at the end of the day.

He was so adventuresome—avoiding injury, yet still managing trouble. He was fearless and loved scaring us—especially our mother.

To him that tall spruce looked perfect from the ground for a Christmas tree. He could see it: decorated with bulbs, ornaments, and tinsel and placed quietly in the living room. 'Rockin' Around the Christmas Tree' playing in the background. He wanted it, and there was no stopping him.

He shimmied up the 40-feet to the top. Almost there and ready to work the saw back and forth, his eyes caught something better right next door. That tree seemed greener, fuller—a much better match for the stockings, Nativity scene and hearth. Moving his body like he was one of our swings in the yard, the trunk began to stir. Our little eyes watched on, our breath forming a fog around our heads. We giggled at his stunt.

Branches and twigs broke free, landing in the snow. He told us to move back out of the way. He was swaying, gaining momentum and now only feet away. Like a frog leaping from his perch above the water, my father sprung, his monkey-like arms clinging and grabbing at anything he could find. We cheered him on, the danger past. For someone like my dad, doing this was easiest. To us, he was unbreakable. We never questioned him. Of course he could jump from tree to tree, suspended high by nothing more than his will not to fall. He was Tarzan on that particular day. But our hero every day.

My mother liked to question him, his tricks unimpressive to her. His antics, his confidence able to upset her like nothing else could. Without her, he'd be dead. She knew this, and he did too. But she loved him all the more for it. And she'd always forgive him, eventually. Even when he burned our field down twice, our barn once.

She was the one behind the scenes. She'd have it no other way. She was quiet, yet confident in raising her children where showing them the Way was easy. She too used the streams, woods, leaves. But mostly, she used her love for animals. She had that special gift of knowing what was needed before anyone else. They connected with her. Pleading eyes showing their thirst, hurt, hunger, contentment. Wounded turtles, cats, and crows all had a better chance when left on her doorstep. Her kitchen floor became a playground for fluffy chicks and tiny mice. My desire and love for animals was evident early on. She never discouraged it. It helped me form compassion and made me aware of more than just myself.

My mother was simple, no nonsense. She didn't need much and raised us simple too. She was always thankful, never expecting anything in return. Staying home to raise us was the most selfless thing she could've done. She was that sturdy force, the one keeping us all on the ground.

Her sacrifice, her servant's heart was that soldier fighting across the ocean for the ungrateful and spoiled back at home. It wouldn't be until I experienced, felt the battlefield first-hand that I realized all she did. And never once complained.

My parent's weren't perfect. But being the first to admit these imperfections was the key to the lock in our upbringing. My dad's seeking of forgiveness with all his physique and manhood was especially huge as a little girl. It would have been easy to keep his heart hidden, withdrawn, and unreachable. He could have allowed his pride to remain as puffed as the throat of a big toad. We probably would've been fooled too.

But he chose something much different for his heart and ultimately ours as well. He chose to wear it everyday on his sleeve, letting us see it first-hand and all it contained. His work came in keeping himself available, sensitive. His humility and gentleness came naturally.

Watching him as a child I witnessed many things. His family came first. Always. I never had to question or wonder about this. We were important and there was nothing we could do to change it. Nothing. He attended my basketball games and school plays and stood watching quietly as I raced Maverick around the barrels in our field. For certain, he was one of my biggest fans.

Concerned about our salvation and relationship with Jesus, he was determined not to 'save the whole world for Christ, yet lose his own kids.' No. He came home every night, tired and dirty yet still willing to be involved. He did it by playing, interacting. He'd ask, then answer the deeper questions.

Ministry to others *was* important. He showed us how to serve. He taught Sunday school to the 1st-3rd graders—his class always a favorite. He was like a big kid telling and re-living the stories in the Bible. We were there with him fighting Goliath with a sling and stone, handing out fish and bread to the people, walking on water during a storm. No one ever wanted to move on from his classroom. Some even sneaked back in for more stories, more adventures. After 30 years, my father still teaches. And is still a favorite.

My parents gave me confidence—just enough to stand firm for what mattered in life. They played out their love story in front of us, never ashamed to kiss and hug against the dishwasher in the kitchen. It'd churn and spray water behind them, unaware while it washed and cleaned our plates and spoons. I tried not to watch. But I was drawn like a pencil to paper. I wanted that. But I also knew I didn't have to go seeking and give myself up to find it.

I knew this because every day they told me I mattered. They meant it when they complimented my outfit. My hair. My sorry skills on the piano. I pounded relentlessly on those white and black keys. I know I caused the whole house some bloody ears.

They were proud of me for no other reason than I was their child. Their blessing. Coming especially from my father, this love caused me to wait. I had his. Nothing else concerned me.

They prayed for us and for our future spouses. They sought godly guidance when it came to the harder stuff. Their faithfulness married to the Lord's grace allowed them to receive blessing after blessing.

At 5, I did something special. I gave my heart to Someone who would keep it safe. He would never throw it away like an empty box or stinky worn out shoes. He would treasure me; even though there would be times I wouldn't treasure Him. It was never He who slapped me across the face, but rather my spoiled hand trying to reach for more in life. I know I stung His cheek.

He guarded me as if I deserved it. I was watched like royalty.

Even at this time of uncertainty with my husband, I knew He was there. I had to hang onto that. A machine beeped from behind, breathing for Graham, bringing me back to his side. I gripped the side bed rail. Cold. It was like that water skiers' handle—the one I was raised on. I never learned that beach start like my mother, but I did learn in the deep, and I grabbed hard waiting for the rushing water to pass over my head. I had to hold my breath for just a few more seconds. I had to wait to pop up on top of water foaming below me, the boat in front of me. My ski steady underneath would keep me going, cutting the water. I just had to hang on. I had to wait.

Rodeo night, July 30th 2010. Graham and Crockett riding in front. Randi is in the back on the paint horse.

Graham ready to rope off Crockett. This is one of the last pictures of Graham before the crash.

Ray Ely and Graham, Summer 2004.

Randi and Maverick, age 9.

Randi and Maverick cooling off in Schroon River.

Family picture taken just weeks before the accident.

Graham is off the helicopter and into
the ER, July 30, 2010.

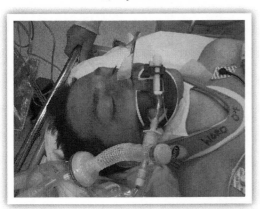

Randi and Graham's wedding anniversary,
August 9th 2010. They celebrated seven years
together in the ICU.

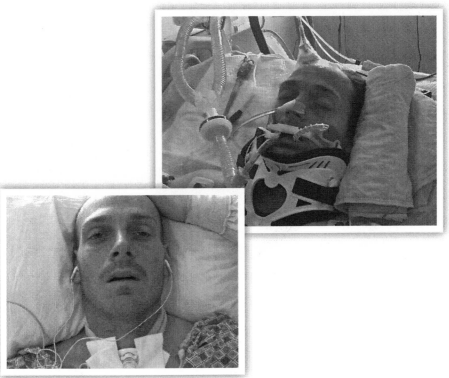

Graham beginning to open his eyes.

Randi's father bare footing on Schroon Lake.

One of Randi's favorite places to sit: next to her Dad in his boat.

Graham and Randi's wedding day, August 9th 2003. Only 20 years old.

Hanging outside The Sunnyview
Rehabilitation Hospital.

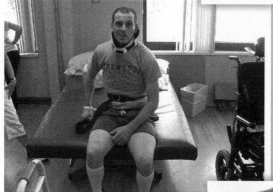

This is the first time
Graham sat up on his own.
Notice the left side of his
face and his arm unable to
help balance.

Walking with lots of help.
Fallon is behind Graham.
His closed eyes remained a
concern for a long time. It was
discovered he had double
vision, a side effect from his
brain injury. He still sees double
with no depth perception today.

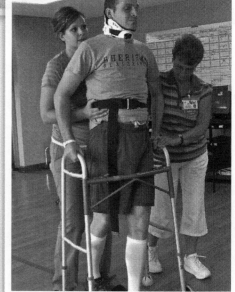

Visit from family. Matt and Abby Vander Wiele.

Randi's parents Keith and Liz Vander Wiele.

Home for just the day. Graham is unaware of
the camera or Wyatt sitting on his lap.

Family taking Graham out of the hospital for a
few hours.

Leaving the hospital for good, September 29th, 2010. Gary and Kathy Stump faithfully stood by their son throughout the entire ordeal.

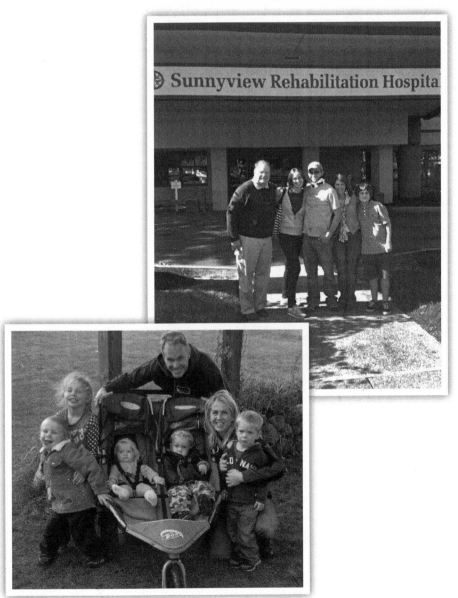

Randi's sister, Bonnie and her husband Dan. They took care their three children plus Graham and Randi's two. All were under the age of 5.

Graham hanging with some family. Dan, Gabe and Matt.

Graham's brother Rick and his wife Jaclyn. This was taken a few months after the accident. While Graham looks fantastic here, he is still very confused and doesn't remember this visit or picture.

There is nothing like sisters. Bonnie is on the left and Renee is on the right. They cried with Randi, prayed with her and helped her through some of her darkest hours.

First time back on Crockett. To this day, Graham feels most
normal on his horse.

Riding the dirt bikes. Graham takes it easy these days, but still enjoys racing his brother-in-law Dan.

Enjoying a family ride once again.

Randi's crazy, loving, God-fearing family.

Fallon Elizabeth Stump,
born April 28th, 2012.

Riding The Dark Stretch together again.

8
REAL VOWS

*'Faith's most severe tests come not when we see nothing, but when we
see a stunning array of evidence that seems to prove our faith vain.'*
~Elisabeth Elliot

That day for us dawned early. The sun was so bright it hurt to
look at the world. Memorizing the smallest details mattered
to me. The chairs and how they sank into the yard, the vases
filled with my favorite wild flowers, blooming and popping on
long tables. I knew I wasn't going to forget any of it.

I was up early, before them all, scrubbing and washing and
blow-drying my way to him. I sat suspended, my hair brushed
and sprayed into place. My face painted with a light brush, soft
colors. I slipped into the dress my mother had made and fingered
my ring. Simple. Ordinary. No diamond rested there. He didn't
have much money. Thoughts of his question to me that night several months ago roamed my mind. A smile reached my lips.

"You're up to something." Late and tired, I was ready for a
goodnight. But his uneasy ways made me stop, wonder.

"Wait here." He was gone and back again, a bowl, hot and
soapy and wet, in his hands.

"What are you doing?" my eyebrows creased with questions.

"Just sit still." He knelt in front, his hands reaching for my ankles.

I realized it too late. Before I could retract them, he tore the socks from my feet and attempted to submerge them in the suds. My feet bent and twisted in a way to make them fit. But it was no use. My toes still hung from the edges, long, unattractive. I was mortified.

The dirty socks, once white, formed a heap of embarrassment to my left. Prayers bounced off the ceiling and back again as I pleaded for a pause button, a chance to regroup.

Instead, I was left in a baggy t-shirt, sweat pants and straggly hair pulled back, the greasy bun mounted on top. There was no escape. The sweat began to build; the room grew hotter than my father's wood stove.

He was saying something. I needed to focus, to remember this moment. And like a shooting star beginning to cross the night sky, he soon grabbed my complete attention.

"Jesus washed his disciples' feet. And in it he showed love, a servant's heart." He kept busy with the wash, taking his time.

"I want to do that for you. I want to show you I love you by serving you. For always."

It grew quiet with only the sound of dripping water returning to the bowl.

"Marry me."

He lifted one foot, now clean. The towel appeared, wrapping, warming. He repeated the process with the other. Watching. Waiting.

And after all the planning and grooming and waiting, we made a promise under the same pine trees I pranced around as a child. Sap, like clear sticky glue beading and forming on old trunks. In front of God, in front of those most important, we vowed our commitment, love, and service to each other. I promised I'd stick by him in sickness and in health. Even in our youth, we meant it. Every word.

Seven years later, I awoke to an empty bed. Fingers gripped the edge of the sheet as I once again dealt with the hell in which I lived. It was always hard to breathe. I had to wait a moment longer than normal, accepting it, feeling the unknown all over again.

"Happy Anniversary, Graham." My whisper floated to my ears. Hot tears rolled down my face brushing the pillow and taking their place among the thousands of others that had fallen there recently.

I forced my legs over the edge of the bed and sat up. My head rolled from the motion. This was not going to be an easy day.

The water in the sink was running full blast, waiting to be used, but I couldn't break from the image staring at me in the mirror.

I didn't even know her. This girl had a puffy face, hollow eyes, swollen nose. She almost looked dead, the light behind her eyes gone. I moved, and she did too. Her head tilted; mine did too. She just kept staring at me.

I filled my hands, water splashing and wetting my face. Rubbing and clawing couldn't cleanse the dirt I thought was there deep in the pores. The kind you can't see, but nonetheless irritating, grating.

I talked to Jesus. Our conversations always going now, always right there. He walked to my dresser with me. He watched me pull a shirt and pants and socks from the old dresser. He sat with me as I continued to cry and dress, pulling one arm through, then the other, my head last.

I tried to apply the make-up that kept running down, smearing a mess. At the same time, He applied love and hope and grace to my heart and soul. He filled it with faith not my own. Whatever was to come this day, this day of anniversary and remembrance, He'd be the one to get me through it.

I had to see Graham, today of all days. Even with it so gloomy and dismal, my expectations could not be dashed. I had to cherish that desire of seeing him healed.

The poking, pinching and squeezing of Graham's fingers, toes, inner thighs, had started producing results. He was feeling those hemostats, pens and fingers. And he didn't like it. His right hand started moving slowly in the direction of the source. But he could never find it. He wanted to swipe, push, fight it off. But, he couldn't. Bruises the color of plums, ripened and dark, were turning a more blue with yellow. And through it all, his left side remained still, unmoving. Like it wasn't even there.

The unicorn man in the bed had gone. His pressure normal, the rod removed. No pieces of head taken. But the woods were far from clear. I signed paper after paper for a tracheotomy and feeding tube. They'd have it done within a few hours. With a shaved head and not so many tubes, he looked cleaned up. He looked like those crazy sets of wires behind the desk all going different ways, now sorted, organized, coiled together. I couldn't wait to see.

I wasn't allowed in. I wasn't allowed to watch. I would've too. Blood and procedures, needles and incisions had always fascinated me. But, the curtain closed and left me standing with my purse, my phone and many doubts about my decisions. A tray lined with instruments, shiny and sharp and sterilized, rolled into his room. I prayed it was right. I prayed the feeding tube and new breathing device were only temporary.

It didn't take long before I had to get out of that hospital.

Guilt clouded my heart. I had to busy my mind, my body. I had been sitting far too long.

Browsing the mall isles for shoes, pants and fresh underwear, I was almost able to rid myself of the sick feeling in my gut. Almost. His siblings gathered clothes and pushed me into dressing room after dressing room.

Other family forced high-sugared coffee drinks into my hands. I quickly became addicted, the more chocolate, whip cream and ice, the better. Regular solid food seemed too heavy, like bricks sinking down, down. What I guzzled down was unhealthy, filled with fake energy, limitless calories, a false sense of hydration. They were perfect.

People meandered alongside me oblivious, unaware.

How were they to know? Could they see my husband lying in a coma in my eyes? Were there others here like me? Loved ones hurt, dying. A machine breathing for them?

I made better eye contact and smiled, thinking my small gift to them could be all they received that day.

I finished my second drink and strode back into his room, anxious to have a look. My few shopping bags hanging out in a nearby car. Graham would've been happy that I actually spent money on myself.

He *did* seem better at least from the outside. A blue tube ran from his neck to the machine breathing for him and another ran from a hole in his stomach to an IV bag filled with a yellowish substance hanging nearby. It was slowly feeding him. Drip. Drip.

A port to his heart was plastered to his triceps. No more searching for veins from his wrists. This would be easier to collect blood, administer medications. Watching the constant poking and prodding was getting old, and it was clear those veins had had enough.

His hair looked like he had been drafted into the Army. Except he was far too frail for boot camp. I could see his face now. But the tubes weren't really gone. Just relocated. He had a sunken in look with high cheekbones, prominent forehead and too big a nose. I hadn't realized how much weight he'd lost already. It was only day 10, the toll taking much from his body.

I shoved earphones into his pink ears while my thumb skimmed through song choices. I smiled. Beyonce, Janet Jackson, all sounded tempting. I settled instead on some good 'ol George Strait shuffled with Pearl Jam and David Crowder.

His parents arrived. Gary liked to stand at the foot of the bed, gripping Graham's feet. He'd look so intensely at his son I could almost hear his pleading soul filled with aggressive prayers to God. He was a pastor; he knew the ropes. It wasn't his first time in an ICU room. He knew this was serious.

Kathy sank into a chair in the corner. She stuffed her oversized purse nearby and pulled a nail file out. The file glided back and forth, up and down, sanding and smoothing her already perfect nails. I glanced at my own. I'd need more than a file. More like a hand sander. The kind used to take varnish off, smooth rough wood. The chances of her having one in that purse were probable—that and any other object one could possibly need to survive for a month.

She liked to read to Graham. Getting to his room some mornings before anyone else, she'd sit, the Psalms pouring from her lips in easy fluidity. Job was his favorite, so she read that one too.

My dad sat in the sun, atop the air conditioner positioned directly behind Graham, a quiet hum cooling the small room. He'd watch the cars, the people below. His perch near the window a bit of an escape. He was that quiet servant in the corner, filling needs before the beckon. He made the phone calls, purchased those ridiculous drinks, the new sneakers helping to sooth the blisters on my feet.

He had a trademark. Something no one else could do. No one could master. My father could console me. Just when I'd crumble with that overwhelmed look plastered on my face, his words brought me back. He'd somehow buckle me back in on this ride I couldn't get off.

The nurse returned, hands working easily to open the yellow liquid from a can. She began pouring. I wondered what it tasted like. And realized if Graham were awake he'd have nothing to do with it. It flowed down the tube and into his stomach so quickly. He surely wasn't able to savor it.

"We'd like the results from his MRI. Is there a Doctor on staff?" Gary wanted some answers.

My eyes flew to the nurse, waiting for a response.

"I'll check for you." She finished the feeding, cranked the tube and adjusted the bag. Then she was gone.

It was go time. Do or die. I'd finally have some answers. Maybe. Even the possibility of answers was a different feeling for me. *Did I really want to hear them?*

A figure moved into the room, an Indian doctor I had seen only in passing. He shook the men's hands, even mine. His name fell from dark lips so easily, so quickly. There was no chance I'd pronounced it back even if my life depended on it.

His demeanor coincided with his intelligence; he had worked hard for the white jacket he wore. Poised, professional, experienced, he reminded me of those hikers—the ones who finally conquered Mount Everest, the most difficult of climbs. Whatever he was, neurologist, neurosurgeon, both, he had arrived.

He leaned against a counter. Sink, paper towels, gloves, all behind him. Eyes dark, like the stethoscope hanging from his neck; moving from Graham, to me, to us all.

"My colleagues and I have discussed the results of his MRI." The accent was thick, yet well versed.

My breath was captive in burning lungs.

"It shows extensive brain damage consistent with what is called Diffuse Axonal Injury or DAI."

A loud beating reverberated in the room, like drums, a djembe. But this was no musical instrument. It was my heart, beating its fastest tempo yet.

Where was he going with this?

"We've known he's had this bruise and some bleeding on his brain, which is serious, but not severe. He really should be waking up by now."

His eyes moved all around the room, to each person, even to Graham who lay listening to music, the machines doing all the work.

"The MRI confirmed what we've thought has been going on."

He paused.

"He has shearing of the brain cells on a microscopic level, and we actually don't expect him to wake up." So matter-of-fact, so final. Like the last nail hammered in a coffin.

Someone must've hooked a vacuum to the room, sucking the air out. I couldn't get in enough oxygen. I couldn't breathe. The room began shrinking, my fingers tingled, and I was losing feeling in my legs. Good thing I was sitting down.

Maybe I heard him wrong. But I couldn't find the words to ask him; those had been taken too.

"What are you telling us, Doctor?" Like me, my dad was struggling to find air too. His voice was hardly above a whisper.

"Oh, he may be able to get off the ventilator and breathe on his own one day. But, most likely, that will be all he can do."

Was that supposed to make me feel better? Where was the good news?

No. There wasn't any. This couldn't be happening. I wasn't ready for this. But I couldn't stop the onslaught. It just kept coming.

"You may want to start thinking about his quality of life because he will most likely continue on in this vegetative state."

The silence was awkward.

I couldn't cry. I couldn't scream. I was frozen in shock. I tried to fight the news like a child swipes at an angry swarm of bees. But the bees wouldn't leave, their numbers increasing with each desperate punch at the air, getting worse and worse. Instead of fleeing for safety, I was trapped here. I couldn't get away from their stings. Deep and sure and sinking into my skin, my heart.

Was he still talking? Still stinging me?

"Brain shearing is usually an after-effect of the initial injury itself, often taking several days to appear. The force of his fall has caused the cells inside his brain to detach from each other, break apart. These cells are the ones that tell him to talk, walk, swallow, eat, live. They do everything for us."

"But some have healed from this, right?" My dad was grasping onto anything he could.

"It's true, some do. And each brain injury is different. But, based on the tests we've done and the extent of his injury, he really only has a 1% chance of pulling through something like this."

"I'm sorry." He looked right at me. He was sincere.

6 months?

The room grew quiet. Awkward. Uncomfortable. It was quickly becoming unbearable.

We were like an audience, the most discomfited of kinds, waiting for the scene to change, for the announcer to come and set things straight. The kind making their way on stage, tapping the mic, one, two times, the feedback causing us to grab at sensitive ears.

My eyes squinted as I tried to make out the figure, the one readying to speak.

Gary. The father of the one lying in that bed, the one who lost his wife all those years ago.

"Well, Doctor." His voice cracked with emotion, and he had to sink a big breath to continue.

It was hard to look at him, the feeling so raw, so real. But we couldn't help it. We were glued to him.

"We appreciate your prognosis and the medical skills you and all the staff bring here." The doctor waited quietly. Gary's tears streamed down, unashamed, unhidden.

"But, you must know, we happen to love and serve the Great Physician. The One who can overrule this prognosis any time He'd like."

He went on.

"We respect your diagnosis, but we don't agree. We can't. This will not be taken as truth."

He was so firm, believing every word from his mouth.

"We'd like to go on record. Graham will walk again. Graham will run again. And he will come back to us, repaired, even better than before."

Graham's chest rose and fell with the force of the machine breathing for him. Gary nodded his head in closing.

"Science can only go so far. And it's in moments like these where miracles must come in." The Doctor was soft. And with no more to say, he dismissed himself.

My head set between my hands, pressing in, holding it together, less it come undone. Hunched over, I tried to make pictures from the grain in the tiles. A face. A cross. Anything. Something pierced the side of my temple.

I pulled my hands away. It was his wedding band.

The longer it spent stuffed on my pointer finger, the lonelier it seemed to become.

His swelling now past, the body acquainted with the endless fluids, I knew what I had to do. I worked the ring from mine.

Somehow I stood. Somehow I made my way to his left side, my hand on his forehead, the other holding his hand. My family: his parents, my dad, all waited, their support overwhelming.

The tears that didn't come with the news were here now. Falling in an endless flow, like leaves on a windy fall day.

The future looked scary, full of missed opportunities, lost plans, vanished goals. It looked cut short. It seemed unfair.

But, I made a promise to him, to us, on this very day, all those years ago. And I planned on keeping it, renewing it, actually living it.

"I love you Graham Stump." My voice was weak, but sure.

"I promised you something that I want to make clear once again, in front of God, my family, yours." I found his ring finger, limp, unfeeling.

"I'm not going anywhere. I'm staying and not leaving. With God's help, His grace, mercy, His love for us; we will get through this." I pushed the ring into place. It slid with easiness, familiarity. Like a magnet returning to the refrigerator, it was back where it belonged. It was home.

I kissed his forehead, hot, clammy. I reached for a wet cloth to wipe it. I had never seen him look so awful. But I had never loved him more.

I ached for our children. The ones we helped make.

"Please, I need to go home. I can't be here anymore." My eyes lifted to see their own tears streaming, an ache so deep the bottom would never be found. Yet, something else was there too. An admiration, an appreciation filled with wonder, awe. They couldn't believe what I had just done.

The car ride home was silent, my dad holding tight to the steering wheel, his face strained and looking aged. I couldn't wait to get home. But, part of me wanted his truck to continue on forever. Maybe if we just kept going, this would all go away. Maybe by the time we stopped for our first fill up this would all be over, and I wouldn't have to face what lay ahead. Everything I saw reminded me of that man, and it'd only get worse the closer we came to our driveway, our home. The one we built together.

How was I going to explain this to our babies? Too young to fully understand, but still wandering for answers. I had never been happier to see them, our boys with knees and smiles and little hands identical to their dad's. A dad I hoped they would someday know.

9
CHEAP RENT

'So many believe that it is love that grows, but it is the knowing that grows and love simply expands to contain it.'
~Wm. Paul Young

The plan was to camp with tents, sleeping bags, a fire, barely edible food. But I was uneasy—not of the wilderness or the coyotes whose fear for me was stronger. I liked adventures but not this kind. The day was melting, and with each drop, my apprehension built as my first night alone with my husband, as his wife, grew near. I had never imagined "this" in a tent, and I couldn't believe he had talked me into it.

Comfort would be hard to come by—the ground a stiff board underneath us. Water would be scarce—the stream a good distance away. The only thing close to us would be the bathroom since any tree did the job.

To make matters worse, it started to rain. I hoped I would be saved from the romantic getaway.

"What do you want to do?" My rising palms exposed the onslaught of rain, trying desperately to hold the wet. Instead, it dripped down my wrists and arms and drenched my shirtsleeves. I stood waiting patiently on my parent's sidewalk while Graham stuffed our things in the trunk of his car just feet in front of me. Most of the guests had long left at the first signs of trouble from the clouds. The tables, chairs and few remaining visitors stayed safe and dry under the tents.

We were just about set, and I could tell he was more than willing than I to venture out into the woods. He was always up for fun, always wanting to experience something new and unique. Thankfully, he knew me better than I thought, his consideration for my wants always foremost on his mind.

"I'll do whatever you want." His hands worked carefully to arrange our things so as not to crush anything. He was wet too with dark spots appearing all over his gray t-shirt.

"Do you have a plan B?" I was hopeful for one but quite sure it didn't exist.

His face said it all. He didn't. "Nope."

The trunk slammed shut. His contagious smile forced my own lips to lift in laughter, and I felt my head shaking in disbelief. He reached for my door handle, and I headed for the open seat. He raced around the front with the rain a soft thud on the roof and windshield. Weary wipers moved back and forth pushing the water off the edges. It had a calming effect.

"We could get a motel room." His seat belt clicked into place; he was staring at me waiting for my decision.

"I don't want to spend the money." I had long since changed from my dress, which now hung carefully in my mother's closet. The only thing still intact from the busy day was my hair, and even that was looking like it had seen better days. It twisted and curled around my face from the humid air and dripping rain. I attempted to tame my locks but was quickly forced to give up. Maybe I'd find time later.

"We *could* go to my apartment." His eyebrows raised in suggestion.

"You mean *our* apartment?" I was waving to the few family and friends seeing us off, their battle with the rain commendable.

"Right, our apartment." The car backed out, turning down the road. Afraid to look at him, I stared out the rain-spotted window like it was my first time driving through the town I had always called home. There was the post office, the one grocery store and gas station. The bank sat almost perfectly in the middle of it all, a coffee shop and church nearby. We were getting close. We passed the pizza place and a few Inns and Bed and Breakfasts all positioned for that beautiful view of our lake.

I had only been in his apartment once to help him move in. Even then, I couldn't believe how only one person could live in such a tight space. It had to be the tiniest apartment in town with 250 square feet. And now I was moving in too.

The rent was cheap: $190 a month. I was going to keep the hallways vacuumed and picked up, dropping the rent to only $160. We could have said no. We could've had a bigger, nicer place somewhere else. But we wanted to save. A house of our own with rooms and space and a yard would have to wait in our dreams for now.

Still, it was going to be tricky. Finding and inventing ways for storage and space and dinners with guests would be a constant challenge. The entire bathroom was the size of a small closet; the pedestal sink was white and short, opposite the shower and in front of the toilet, so we weren't able to fit at the same time. We would have to take turns unless he stood in the shower to brush his teeth while I washed my face. That could work. Either way, we'd have to work out some kind of system. I was thankful it'd at least be quick and easy to clean.

He pulled into his regular spot front and center. He popped the car into park. I soon found myself walking up the old rickety steps, each one producing a different sound, the tune of our arrival. No one ever told me this huge boxy building had once been a chicken coop, now renovated for people to live in. He held the front door for me to pass. It looked worn and heavy. The walls were thin, old and needing paint. An unwelcome smell met my nose, cigarette smoke and musty carpet mixed with other unspeakables. The additional tenants had to know we were here. I gripped my bag and continued up the stairs trying to push my nerves back down them. They stayed with me all the way to his door.

Hands dipped into a pocket for the key produced nothing. Undeterred, he pulled an old grocery store rewards card from his wallet. Its intended use I knew had been ignored, but it became apparent it served him well in other ways. The slightly bent, worn and cracked plastic fit perfectly between the door and the lock. With one magical finagle, it blew open like a soda top.

My mouth must've been open. And it must've been written all over my face.

"It's okay. It's usually not that easy to open. I got lucky this time." His smile disappeared inside. There I was left standing in the hallway with my bag, a few presents and my nerves. I gathered them up and moved toward the door jam. I peered in, hesitant.

It was smaller than I remembered—the kitchen more like a kitchenette, the kind you see in campers, small RVs. I didn't even see the refrigerator until I caught the harvest gold color seeping from a crack in the door. There was no counter space and only two cupboards above the stove, two burners, and an extra small oven. One drawer would have to hold all our kitchen utensils.

This area was the same space we would use for sitting and eating. A window allowed some light, but it was going to need curtains. And soon. A small table sat underneath the pane with matching chairs, old, weary. I knew no matter how I moved and twisted that table, there would only ever be room for two.

It was obvious he had not cleaned or prepared anything for my arrival. We were supposed to be out in the woods by now pitching our tent, starting a fire. Now, I wasn't sure which was worse: the tent with the wet rain or this.

His fly-fishing gear hung suspended on the wall with nails and hooks. The rod, vest, and net all spaced perfectly and easy to get to. It was his only wall décor if you could call it that.

The top of the fridge acted as a shelf, which held a jar of loose change, dusty and dirty. There was something else up there too, but I couldn't make it out. A recliner type chair sat in the only available corner, a tall light standing behind. I understood this to be the living room, right next to the table, across from the sink and just two short steps from where I stood. We'd have to share that recliner, with a tear in the armrest, the threads protruding like whiskers on a cat.

This was where he sat, totally engrossed, attacking a wedding present like he was 5 again, vigorous, excited. Head bent, fingers ripping at paper, the pieces falling near his feet. That small amount of paper made the entire area appear messy, unkempt. Like post-Christmas morning, with paper dumped everywhere, boxes without their lids, bows and string tangled in the middle of it all.

I hadn't even made it past the opening when he glanced my way.

"I don't have much silverware here. So, I grabbed this box from the pile. It just felt right."

Was he more nervous than me?

I watched him pull the set from the box. The exact ones he had shot with that gun to put them on our list. My mind wandered, wondering what he'd been eating with all this time.

He cut the ties holding them together with his pocketknife. Snap. They were loose, a new life awaiting them nearby. He pulled the drawer and dropped them in. No organizing. No washing them first. Not even a rinse. The drawer squeaked shut.

He turned. Nerves I had never seen traced his face. I *knew* it.

It was my turn to say something.

"Are you going to invite me in? Or were you planning on opening presents all night?" I started to enjoy his discomfort.

"I'm such a jerk. Can you tell I'm nervous?"

"Yeah, actually I can."

I glanced to the right and spotted his room; being only a few feet away, it was hard to miss. His dresser stared back at me, drawers open, clothes spilling out. We would be sharing the full-sized bed with crumbled sheets and blankets. My belongings would fit at the foot in a dresser stacked carefully atop two end tables. It reminded me of the game 'Jenga' with wooden pieces carefully put in place, pulled out, stacked and re-worked. I didn't want any of this to come crashing down. It wouldn't be so easy to set back up again. I was glad we didn't have much and welcomed the challenge before me—one with cramped space and tight quarters. We wouldn't be surviving on much more than love. But that was good enough for us.

After all this time, I could finally call him mine. My husband, my partner in this life we now shared together. I had to learn him. Study him. See what made him tick. At times, he tested me; his laid back ways were a crash course to my taskmaster personality disorder. He preferred the journey with that slow drive taking in the beauty around him, the mountains, the leaves, the streams. The destination wouldn't matter much for him, more like a side dish on his plate—there because it had to be. Of course, this mentality would make him late to everything. And it was sure to cause some conflict seeing I was raised to be five minutes early. Still, he'd persist in getting me to see life as he did, to enjoy my travels, capture the sights, hear the sounds, revel in the feel. Just like him.

I knew thoughts swam their way around his brain, even when he promised they didn't. He claimed he was like all the others. But I knew better. He *was* different. He was even. Simple. Well-rounded. And I knew I wouldn't be able to change him. There'd be no speeding him up. Or slowing him down. He marched to his own drumbeat, the one thumping inside his head. His quick wit and charm would keep me on my tip-toes, reaching ever higher to see over the top.

He wouldn't make any of this marriage stuff easy on me, pushing me to think, perceive, to know what I believed in. He'd know just how to place me where I'd need to be, firm, yet sweet, like the horses he trained.

It'd end up being those horses, the ones where I worked, that'd be his favorite pastime. We planned to spend all our free time with them, working, sweating and riding those needing more for the kids. He excelled at it. His ability to read a horse was a gift. One not many had. He understood them, how they thought, worked. And they favored him. Learning easily from this talent he possessed.

I didn't realize that through the years, he was going to change right before my eyes. Like the headstalls he carved and tooled out of leather, he'd become a finished product ready to be put to use. He'd watched every horse training video, read every magazine. The pages worn and ripped where they had been flipped and turned, pressed and moved.

He'd learn fast, an educated student who soaked up information like a child at story time hour. He wouldn't be afraid to try things for himself; to see what worked and what didn't, always adding his own twists, his unique methods. He wouldn't end up just training horses, or even riding them.

He'd dance with them.

Each step and each move thought out, practiced and perfectly created to form a masterpiece. He'd become more than just my cowboy. Somehow, almost overnight he'd transform into a horseman.

Unfortunately, riding horses wasn't going to pay the bills.

His hands worked hard to provide, showing the dark stain of grease and oil and dirt. He had learned that unique ethic from his father, the kind hardly found anymore. He worked for the family business even before he had claimed me. He installed, replaced, and fixed heating systems, air conditioners and other things that I would never fully grasp. Knuckles bore scars and nicks and scrapes, bleeding and scabbing regularly from a loose piece of metal, the slip of a tool. Even his fingernails, short and chewed down couldn't escape the life he now lived. Black cuticles and punished nails looked almost painted some days. But he loved it. This was the one he wanted, and he'd never complain. Rather, I knew he took his role of providing and putting food on the table seriously. He dreamed of one day building a house all his own. One for me to enjoy. One for all the kids we talked about having. I believed him when he said he was happy in his blue collar. And I knew he was happiest with me.

Truly, I was the lucky one. The one honored to be his. Graham didn't let many in. He was afraid of losing them, having them taken too soon. His past had been filled with a tragedy no child should have to suffer. Still, the loss of his mother helped make him the man he needed to be.

It made him wise, grounded and aware of all things eternal. I would never hear him once blame God. And he never wallowed in self-pity. He simply lived each day as his last. Like it was the final show, the closing ceremony.

While I knew I'd have to study and research him, I was an easy subject for him. He wouldn't have to examine me long to get a good grade. I wore my heart just like my father had on his own sleeve. Except this was my shirt now, my sleeve. My parent's simplicity and country outlook on life was deeply impressed into my soul. He respected what my parent's had done in me, making him love me all the more.

Like my own mother, I didn't need money or things to know how much I was loved or wanted. This craggy apartment, this life I chose, was perfect for me. For us.

I starred back at him, so much to learn, so far still to go. He had picked up my sorry bag, the one I brought for our first week of married life together. He was waiting patiently. No more nerves. No more unease. Just a pure and simple love. We were only kids. I would learn that where I missed in life, he caught. Where I lacked, he abounded. And when I couldn't hear the tempo of life anymore, getting sucked too deep into duties, obligations, tasks and stress, he was always there helping me feel the beat, the rhythm all over again.

10
THE HORSE IN ME

'By reason of his elegance, he resembles an image painted in a palace, though he is as majestic as the palace itself.'
~Emir Abd-el-Kader

They're an old fascination. One hardly satisfied. A hold the same as a fever grips us and forces us into a captivity we can't control. We are spellbound by their power, mesmerized by their beauty and speed. And unaware of their influence, we keep coming back, wanting more of them and all they offer.

Their bodies designed for agility and strength fit us perfectly, flawlessly. We belong on them. And yet we don't. One misstep and we're done. One bad move and it's over. We feel their chests, their lungs filling and pushing air back out with huge breaths, warm and deep. That smell, all their own, covers a soft muzzle, spindly whiskers protruding haphazardly. And we can't get enough. Tender eyelids provide a soft cushion for our lips to rest; a carefully placed jaw line stretches much of their face, showcasing the herbivore lifestyle. Those large eyes carry the shape of steep mountains inside, ones you wish you could climb. Perhaps if you could you'd understand. You'd finally see.

Ears prick like a salute, side-to-side, backward and forward, never missing a sound. The body is muscled, rippling and flexing with each movement, change. Hips rest the same height as the withers, allowing them to turn and stretch out. And a secret hides back here, the key to the lock of supremacy, the source of it all. The ability to brake, speed up and turn on a dime starts from the powerhouse in the back.

They are grace. They are majestic. They are horses. They will take your breath away. The bond unique and as fitting as your own fingerprints, like that of a horseman's gentle touch with the one he calls his own. The horse he's trained, the long hours and wet saddle pads are a true testament of all their hard work together.

Now they are a special treat. Their glamour and intrigue are different than when they used to be needed for survival. We have moved from the necessity and embraced their luxury. We've come a long way, our history inter-locking like a braided rug.

The wild mustangs are the exceptional ones now, protected and preserved on land meant only for them. Hardy and resilient, they're still a prey animal, hunted and chased for food, filling the bellies of wild pups and coyotes. Only the fittest survive, forcing the old, young and sick to the top of the menu. They run first and think later, oftentimes forcing them to become their own worst enemy. Unnecessary havoc and injury come mostly from their own reactions, their own response. Still, they run. It's all they know. And if they can't run, they fight but only as a last resort, a last attempt for survival. Sometimes the fighting works, but mostly the running saves them.

Their numbers allow for safety as they roam and search and sift through the terrain for water and food like vultures, nomads.

But they have no resting place. No place to call home. Young move quickly to keep up, learning their gift of speed within a couple hours, hair just newly dried. They don't want to be left behind. Leadership comes from the matriarch mare, one of the oldest in the group. (¹) Her decisive ways help protect and carry the herd to safety. To grasslands. To water.

Her actions motherly, she shows a tenderness by nudging and tucking and caressing. But, she disciplines too with bites and kicks so loud you can hear them reverberate across the plains. One can only imagine the sting they create and the future obedience they instill. Her actions are never wrong. The herd respects her and follows her lead.

Still, it's a hard life for the wild horse with no guarantees. No security. No promise of a future. They're not left with much more than their elaborate senses and robust hooves to carry them through to another day. Hopefully.

The rest of them, the lucky ones kept in barns, corrals, fields and fences sometimes stretching for miles as they graze for pasture during the long winter months have a much different life where humans care for them. We've taken them from auctions, sales, sometimes plucking them from those wild ways and everything once familiar. We give them a new life, expecting something better for them. Something used for our benefit. Our cause. Our desires. Our motives.

While their instincts are the same as that of the wild mustang, we are a type of arranged marriage for them. Our attempts at pursuing, wanting, loving, spending our hard-earned money, doesn't come natural for them. We're the ones in control. If left in

---

1   Monty Roberts, <u>The Man Who Listens to Horses</u> (London, Great Britian: Random House UK, 1996), pp.18-20.

the pasture, they would stay there. Forever. Not caring one way or the other.

As their keepers, we've mastered the art of domesticating them. We brush them. We feed them. We cinch and un-cinch and throw countless pads, saddles, and harnesses to their backs. They are a business. They are a love. They make us mad by testing our patience like only a horse can, each different from the other with personalities as big as their size. But they make us happy too, filling voids and hiding deep scars dug there by our own kind.

A mind-boggling athlete, we've trained them to spin, race, jump, collect and trail-ride right into our hearts. One minute a fierce competitor jockeying for position, the next that gentle kitten, giving rides to children and those disabled.

And they finally have a purpose, a reason because someone decided to put work into the horse, picking them, choosing them. For some, it's to buck cowboys off at high school rodeos. For others it's to run big and jump high, the ribbons and trophies many. Both are needed. Both supply our interests.

My entire life led up to the moment Graham entered the coma. And I was haunted with the image of his head ricocheting on the arena floor, the dust rising as smoke left only ashes for me to sift through.

I was a wild horse; the one pressed around the round pen, running circles in a desperate plea to escape. Scared and lost and sweating under the stress. The unknown the most difficult to accept, I bucked and reared and fought against the will laid out before me. His will. My sides heaved hard from exhaustion, my thirst more than I could bear. I was lost, uncertain, and desperate for the meaning, the purpose to it all. Like squirrels gathering for a long winter, my eyes moved here then there, shifting franticly for an answer, for help.

I traveled round and round. Sure of nothing.

But in the center of that pen, a circular pattern with worn edges, the ground damaged from my flighty hooves, a figure stood. I had never seen anything like Him. His stance and demeanor was calm, but I remained fearful and distant. I was certain He was out to get me. He watched me like a pack of wolves do the wild herds or lions do zebras on the African plains. I waited for Him to jump, claws outstretched for the kill, sinking into my delicate flank. He was going to eat me. It'd be a slow death too, suffocating and choking. For me, there was no other choice. I had to keep going, running for my life. But even the best horse can't run forever. I'd soon grow tired and have to accept my fate, my impending death. I braced for the attack.

But it didn't come. I felt nothing. The claws didn't spring out, sharp and thick. The teeth were not thrashing. Rather, He communicated with me, wanted my attention. I couldn't make out the words, foreign and strange to my ears. Still, I felt He would have answers, the reasons for this discomfort. I honed in on Him, observing, watching Him; running all the while. Questions skirted my mind as my hooves lifted off the ground, truly flying at times.

Why were we here? And what did he want? Where did my nice life go? Where was all that grass I had just been chewing on moments before? Where was my herd of friends? My security? I was barn sour wanting only to go back to what was safe, what I knew, where I thought I belonged.

It became clearer to me than the river stone lying low at the bottom of the brook, water rushing fast over its surface. I had lessons to learn here, my instincts the same as all those young and wild horses entering their own round pen for the first time. I was now looking through their eyes, the horse in me.

He had brought me here, choosing and plucking me from all I had known. And I didn't know why. My life, my breeding was pathetic, a 'grade' as they say, like a mutt with no famous blood pulsing through my veins. I had nothing to offer. Nothing to give. I was worthless. Good for nothing. I'd be best put out in the pasture. A decorative lawn ornament.

But He wanted something. And He wanted it badly. He craved it. Desired it. And like an obsession, He had to have it. 'He went up on the mountainside and called to Him those whom He desired. And they came to Him.' (Mark 3:13 ESV)

It was simple. He wanted *me*. All of me. A relationship with me. Intimate. Deep. One I'd never known before. All I had to do was come. And it was time. Time for me to trust. Time for me to yield.

I stopped my running, faced Him and met His eye for the first time. I needed Him, His leadership. I needed His help to survive this and like the wild mustang seeks the matriarch mare for guidance, I looked to Him. My Teacher. My Trainer.

I was finally ready to begin. Me with all my wild mess. And Him with those hands, the ones with scars the shape of a jagged circle. He had knowledge and experience. He had done this before. He'd push. He'd ask. He'd apply pressure, and when I'd get it right He'd release it as quick as it came. This was the same kind horse trainers apply to a young one in training. Most of the time, it hurt. And I didn't like it. But I had to go through it. He was preparing me, training me for something special. Something for His benefit. His glory.

Would the hours invested pay off? Would I remember these lessons? The repetitions, the practice? Soon it'd be show time. My saddle would have to be oiled, my blankets cleaned, my mane combed perfectly to one side, the Sho-Sheen thick and shiny on my coat. Would I be willing? Would I truly trust Him to lead me safely through the scariest time of my life? Did I even want Him to?

I was tempted to spook and carry on. Old habits die hard. This was all so new to me, objects loomed everywhere, ones I had never encountered before. It was scary and unknown. The one afraid to cross a puddle, I danced my hooves this way and that, thinking surely the water would swallow me whole. I didn't know it was only a few inches deep.

Slowly, He began gaining my trust. With each lap around that round pen, I started to understand His words to me. I allowed Him to show me, mold me, turn me this way, that way and back me in a straight line. He threw ropes and bags, blankets and finally a saddle at me. He was desensitizing and sensitizing all at once. His touch was gentle and kind, one all good horse trainers know about. The rub along the neck, the pat on the shoulder, the caress between the eyes. Horses know this touch and trust it. It calms, it soothes, it encourages, it speaks the same words. Words of comfort. Words of reassurance. For me, this touch trickled into my mind, my heart, my soul.

Eventually He climbed confidently into the saddle, sinking deep and sure, flexing my head and neck from side to side, making certain I had it down. He asked me to step, to move off his leg, his cue for the first time. Together as a team. As one. I didn't know where I was stepping exactly, what I was doing or what was happening to me. But He knew me better than anyone—my abilities, potentials, limitations.

Before He brought me to this round pen, this trial with Graham, The Dark Stretch, He had watched me. Every good horse trainer does it, and He was no different. He knew just how I'd flit across the paddock, how I'd handle that lead change, that go. That stop. If you know horses, really know them, you'd know the importance of this simple act, the feat of observing the horse naturally before adding the saddle. A rider.

The way they position those legs, shoulders and head are all clues, pieces to the puzzle inside them. Knowing this, you'd never ask the horse to do something you know he couldn't do, something he wouldn't be able to handle.

A Quarter horse can't win the Kentucky Derby. And you'll never see a Draft or Clydesdale performing in an eventing competition.

He knew what I could handle and what I couldn't. He wasn't going to ask too much of me. He had wired me from the beginning—formed me in my mother's womb. Created me. I was the passenger, not Him. He was the one holding the reins, and for that I was thankful. He'd be at every show, every race, every rodeo. He wasn't going anywhere. He'd never leave my side. He'd go over every rail and perform every dance in the dressage ring with me. While I was terrified to continue, my heart beating like those of hummingbird's wings, I would listen to His commands. I had to follow His lead in my life. There was no other option. I depended on Him completely now. I wouldn't be able to survive on my own anymore. My wild life quickly became a distant and dark past.

There was no way I'd be able to take credit for my fast spins, my long slides or high jumps. He would win the points, the money in the end. Remember, He had picked me. *Me.* Without Him, I'd still be scraping through to the next day, hoping I'd make it. Hoping I could keep outrunning my predators, their mouths watering at the possibilities. He wanted more for me than to just survive The Dark Stretch. He wanted me to run it. Race it. Perform it. Learn from it. The faith I'd need to make it to the end came from Him alone. Him and all His training in my life. Him, His perfect plan, His love running deeper than I would ever truly know.

11
A SURGEON IN THE ROOM

'When you reach the end of your rope, tie a knot and hang on.'
~Abraham Lincoln

August 9th, 2010

I received devastating news today concerning Graham. And I write this with a very heavy heart. Honestly, I feel like vomiting. But I need to plead with everyone who reads this to storm Heaven's gates with me for a complete recovery for Graham. They did an MRI yesterday on him and I was there today when they gave me the results along with my dad and his parents. They have told me there is A LOT of brain damage. They don't expect him to wake up, and if he does he won't be very functional other than being able to breathe on his own.

As you can imagine, my world has come crashing down on me. My faith and trust in the Lord is being tested now more than ever, and I just can't believe what they are telling me. I want to believe in the great Physician, and we will continue to do our best to place moment by moment in his hands, believe the Doctors are wrong on this one, and pray that Graham will come back to me fully recovered. They have told me that the most progress is done in 6 months and if in 6 months he is still *sleeping I will need to make a decision about his quality of life. I am living a nightmare and am in a very scary place in my life right now. Please pray for Graham and me. I am crazy about that guy and don't know how I would do this without him. Thank you for your prayers for us. I will keep you all posted as best I can.*

I continued through all kinds of motions. Eating. Dressing. Brushing my teeth. Playing with the kids. My sister and her husband, with small kids of their own, moved in to care for our children. I knew without family, I wouldn't be able to move forward—Bonnie became the mom I couldn't be. She quietly nurtured and cared and selflessly served while at the same time Dan became the father they didn't have. I'd never be able to thank them enough.

Most surprisingly, a kind of routine settled in. A 'new normal' as they say. Kids are the most resilient of kinds. They knew something wasn't quite right, the absence of their father a constant question to ask. But mostly this was a kind of party for them. Cousins and family smothered them with kisses, hugs and the love that we couldn't give them. It helped ease the pain. It helped erase the questions.

It was far from a party for me, and I remained amazed at all I could experience and still continue.

Even a broken heart keeps beating. Numb legs somehow continue to walk. Your lungs are forced to find each breath as you suck it in and back out. Again. And again. You drink. You eat. You become full on even the smallest amount of fuel. Your body continues while your soul rives in pain. Sometimes I was peering in from the outside, my body like a shell, a robot. Other times I was in the heat of every emotion pummeling my way, every nerve in overdrive, every feeling harsh and overdrawn.

I was prepared for the worse. My practical senses suggested I be ready for his death. A vegetative life. But even my own mind couldn't make me give up hope. I refused to. I clung like spider monkeys cling to their mothers' backs. A tight grasp full of hair and skin ensuring their place, their safety net while their mothers trudge through deep waters or climb steep trees. I hung onto the possibilities. I clutched to the power of prayer. I wished for a modern-day miracle. I tried to stay positive.

But it remained hard. My optimism was drifting in a sea of dire and tragic information without a lifejacket or floating device. It seemed only a matter of time before it would sink, becoming engulfed by waters it wanted nothing to do with. Science, medicine, and doctor's notes seemed to battle against any act from God, a possible phenomenon from Him. Who knew more? Whose research had the most data? The most facts? The most practical meaning to it all? And which was I going to ultimately believe? The tests, results and statistics? Or that God truly had Graham in the palm of His hand, ready to fulfill a plan for his life?

Sometimes it would've been easier to simply accept what they were telling me. To allow my lungs to fill with those dark waters of cynicism and gloom.

Perhaps drowning was the way to go.

"Are you ready for report?" It was a doctor. I turned to have a look, the perfectly cleaned glass easy to see through. I wondered how they managed to avoid the streaks and smudges. They must've had good cleaners. That and the absence of children with dirty fingers and sweaty palms an unspoken blessing. This doctor wasn't Indian, rather very American-looking. He looked middle-aged with a goatee-peppered red with a bit of white. He had a wife; my eyes caught his gold wedding band glistening against his freckled hand. I only assumed he had two kids. Probably one boy and one girl. The perfect picture of the American dream come true.

I reached for my purse from underneath my chair. I knew I should leave. But I waited a moment too long, hoping they'd shut the door. That's what they usually did when family was around. They'd either ask us to kindly go to one of those dreaded holding cells or politely slide the perfect, see-through glass doors shut, blocking and avoiding any chances of eavesdropping.

"Yes, I'm ready." Graham's nurse stood just outside the door, a notebook in her hands. *She must have forgotten I'm here. Perhaps I was sitting too still. Could they really not see me?* My eyes caught the curtain, the one designed to be pulled and yanked while Graham was being changed or worked on. It was tugged a different way today. A way that allowed me to see them, yet it was clear they couldn't see me.

I froze. *Should I get up? Should I clear my throat to warn them someone was here?* I wasn't just anyone either, I was the wife. His wife.

"How's he doing today?" He glanced over Graham with piercing eyes, ones I would never forget. He started at the feet and worked them up quickly over Graham's legs and upper body until finally resting on his head. His eyes held no hope for his patient, and I couldn't help it, my mouth started to take in some water. I moved my own eyes to Graham. He was gray today, fighting a fever, and his breathing was scaring me.

"He *is* breathing a bit better on his own, but it's so fast." She was whispering. She *did* know I was here. For some reason, she chose to let me continue to listen on.

"We need to make sure we're not sugar-coating his condition to the family." He was scribbling something down, most likely with his favorite pen.

"This is a pretty severe brain injury. It's throughout both frontal lobes and it's not looking good for him." He didn't make eye contact with the nurse. He was too busy writing.

"They *do* seem to be a very religious family." The nurse added with her whispers again. This caused the doctor to look her square on. He clicked his pen shut and found it a home in the top left pocket of his jacket. It rode there like a spoiled Chihuahua in a flamboyant purse.

"That's good. What are they, Latter-Day Saints?"

"I don't think so." She paused, her weight shifting from side to side, her notebook still clutched to her chest. "I think they're Baptist or something like that." It was a timid response. One unsure of his reaction.

He looked up immediately. She had his full attention and there was a thick silence. Only the all too familiar beeping of machines met our ears. I was too afraid to breathe for fear of being found in this chair I was surely glued to by now. I couldn't get up even if I tried.

"Well, they're going to need that in order to get through this." He sighed and rolled his chair to the right, toward his next patient. He grabbed at his Chihuahua pen and spoke more words to the nurse that I couldn't hear.

My jaw ticked and pulsed from fighting back the roller coaster of emotions. But it was no use; my eyes pooled with tears that cascaded down much like the waterfalls do over rocky cliffs. I truly was drowning, taking on way too much water. I could feel my head slipping under the cover of wetness, my lungs about to burn out and breathe their first gulp of water. Things would soon grow dark, and I hoped it wouldn't hurt for too long. I closed my eyes, the blackness shielding me from what lay on the other side. I was about to welcome it in, allow the dark shadows of doubt and pessimism to become my new best friend.

But there was something I couldn't forget. Something that made my eyes fight open, my head shake free of its prison.

There were so many praying for Graham—prayers for his healing and recovery. His name like a lollipop to their tongue, stuck and fixed there. Some were even praying for me that I'd have the strength to believe and continue on, that with His power I'd get through this somehow. Even just one prayer could not go unnoticed, but there were many. God had to be hearing them. And since He *was* hearing them, He had to be here. He had to be right by that bedside. Right next to Graham.

My head popped above the water, and I lifted it in defiance. My lungs sucked in new air, deep and sure. I made up my mind and pushed Satan with all his lies, his doubt and dark creepy waters from the small room. I was going to believe today. I didn't know what tomorrow would bring and perhaps the seas would threaten again. But for now, in this moment, no doctor or nurse, machine or new CAT scan was going to change my heart.

I could feel His presence. And it warmed me. He was here, perhaps even standing by Graham's bed. It made my thoughts run wild with imagination and what-ifs. I couldn't help but day-dream. Images danced like clouds forming picture after picture through my mind. Things I couldn't see with my own eyes but nonetheless there. Hidden. Behind the scenes. I just knew it.

I saw their fingers first like veterans of war moving and jos-tling with accomplishment and strength, their touch of experience evident. And smooth. This wasn't their first go-around or battleground march. Medals of achievement and honor hung confidently above on stiff and starched surgical gowns, their numbers too many to count. Being the most qualified of hands, I imagined their skill as top-notch. Unmatched ability still gentle and tender with their work.

There were four of them total, two pair. Their hosts, two figures of similar height stood on either side of Graham, his head sandwiched between their gowns. I could barely make out their eyes; facemasks and surgical hats covered most everything with that breathable blue material. Still, I didn't miss what I saw, the brightest of eyes. Deep. There was wisdom there. Discernment I would never have.

They were busy sorting through something, heads bent in concentration and focus. I saw cells, mixed up wiring and jumbled messages all spilling haphazardly from Graham's head. Even I could tell they weren't right. The wires popping and squirming like a garden hose with too much pressure and no one manning it. It looked a mess. It looked unrepairable.

The one on the left lifted and moved things carefully. It looked like He was putting a puzzle back together. The kind with a million pieces, daunting, and overwhelming, spread out on a huge kitchen table. But nothing here was intimidating to Him. He was making it all appear easy with no hesitation in finding that next piece to add to the bigger picture. It was child's play for Him.

The figure on the right waited patiently for instructions. I realized he was the helper, the one aiding and assisting. I imagined him as the angel. But he still had a busy job of holding, grasping, gripping neurons and cells, waiting for the head Surgeon's final touch of healing. He held a big bundle now, quietly standing in place. Only the Surgeon knew the exact spot and placement of each cell. Only He could heal and fix this collection of brokenness. This disorder.

There were no sounds of the shiny and sterilized metal clipping open and closed. No trays stood balanced and lined with gauze and bowls and other dressings. No instruments were needed. Just those gentle hands. No medical team stood waiting in their scrubs in case of an emergency. There were no headlights or overheads hanging suspended like chandeliers. Light was there on its own, like it couldn't help it. Like it belonged here with this Surgeon. The two of them worked quietly. They worked without anyone even knowing they were here. But I knew. I could feel them.

"This piece needs your attention." It was the bundle the angel held. It was just out of my view.

"Indeed." The Surgeon finished what He had started and turned His attention to this new area of concern. He fingered it carefully, a brow creasing in thought. He paused only slightly to examine this mass—cells, axons, neurons all needing to connect to work properly again. I was certain it was scrambled chaos.

I imagined His lips moving in a private conversation. One even the helper was left out of. This was with Someone else. Someone He knew better than anyone. Someone He needed, like a best friend, a family member, a Father. I realized He was talking with Himself. The most intimate of prayers.

His hands placed what they held gently back inside my husband. Would it be perfect? Would it be as it once was? No. There on the edge, the last piece slipping into place, a small scar lay.

Perhaps a reminder. Perhaps like Jacob and his wrestle with the Lord, a souvenir. A keepsake. One The Great Physician wanted Graham to carry.

12
NOTEWORTHY TRICK

'For three things I thank God every day of my life: thanks that he has vouchsafed me knowledge of his works; deep thanks that he has set in my darkness the lamp of faith; deep, deepest thanks that I have another life to look forward to—a life joyous with light and flowers and heavenly song.'
~Helen Keller

Why it was allowed I couldn't say. Why it happened I wouldn't know. Not of the accident itself, the looming whys and hows of that already put into play. Out of my line of vision. It was those other questions that tapped at my heart's walls like a woodpecker searching to fill that endless hunger call.

Why *hadn't* he been taken home? Why was he allowed breath when others had been forced to take their last? Tap. Tap. Why?

The rat-tat-tat of its beak, the vertical suspension of body clinging effortlessly is a bird with bright feathers, dark spots, or more simple markings. He takes careful aim. His powerful beak pecking and digging for that which he seeks, his skull thick and able to handle the continual pounding. It's a talent. His profession. And sooner or later he gets what he's so desperately looking for. A sticky tongue reaches and grabs at the bugs, ants, and worms hiding just under the bark. They always meet a quick death. My fill however, wouldn't come so easy. There'd be no simple answers. No easy meal. What I sought was deeper than the thickest tree trunk, my beak coming up just short of my prey. That which I hunted I wouldn't get. Not this side of Heaven anyway.

I could've been over-thinking it. Analyzing the whole thing with too much obsession. It was probably so simple, a piece of God's will, part of His plan. A bit of that bigger picture I couldn't yet see. Either way, it began happening. Like vines creeping up a terrace slow and sure, it took hold almost overnight. There'd be no stopping their path as they traversed up, across and back again. I knew those prayers, the pleas for Graham's life dug deep and produced results. I felt it somewhere within the cavernous parts of my soul, that place no one knows about, no one can see.

The extended forecast the Doctors had so carefully lain out with blizzard conditions complete with an icy mix painted itself rather into a partly cloudy day with only light rain. My husband having been in a coma for three weeks slowly began to lift his eyelids. They would raise and peer out for us to see, sometimes only for a few seconds. But I had to believe in that Surgeon, the One I imagined in Graham's room. Gentle and skilled hands giving him another shot at life.

Thinking Graham would be able to recognize or focus on me, I'd lean close, gaze square on and try desperately to grasp his attention. It wouldn't have mattered if I were looking at an empty wall with eyes painted to match his exactly. There was no expression visible to me. No recognition. His blank stare was almost worst than having them closed. At least with them closed he gave the essence of simple sleep. These were unblinking. Unknowing.

Completely unaware. The eyes I had once been so attracted to now frightened me, looking nothing how I remembered.

He'd twitch his toes from time to time. But his arm, his right hand moved the most. It had a mind all its own as it'd go over and up and all around. It felt his back brace, his neck brace and would swing this way and back again. His hand was the only thing working somewhat normally. But like a horse needing to be tied to a hitching post, the animal forced to stay put and out of trouble, so his arm became as they fastened it to the bed rail. A white strap holding it secure. He clearly wasn't going anywhere. And he didn't like this arrangement.

His collapsed lungs were inflated one last time with some sort of medical apparatus and finally worked as they should. He soon drew his own breath from the hole in his neck, the ventilator rolling from his room on steady wheels when they were sure he had it down. The high fever causing pneumonia and other problems soon dissipated completely. His color even looked better, and he was placed in a recliner-type chair for a couple hours a day.

"You've got to see his trick!" Graham's nurse was standing in the doorframe like her only job was to wait for us to arrive for the day. She was short and sweet and as excited as a child in a candy store.

"His trick?" Rick was with me today, Sarah too. Graham's older siblings were never far from his side. There was something about their baby brother being in the ICU that didn't sit well with any of them. We picked up our pace passing the front counter on one side of us, the patients' rooms on the other. Behind the counter several secretaries sat on swivel chairs, papers strewn and phones cradled between ears and shoulders. Warm smiles welcomed us as they chatted and discussed medical information.

I wondered if it ever got old. The part of their day where death was an everyday occurrence, the language depressing, the news sometimes devastating to relay.

The patients lay just like they always were each morning I arrived. One in particular I couldn't help but become somewhat attached to. He was young, like my Graham with wavy, brown hair. He was only two doors down from us and had come here shortly after we had. He sported the same equipment as my husband, even that metal rod with the shaved top section of hair. But that had been removed days ago. I could only assume he had sustained a head injury, the signs similar in too many ways. I didn't know the extent of his injuries nor how he had gotten here. My guesses were all I had to go on. I'd pass his parents occasionally in the halls, their hollow stares all too familiar to me.

Today his curtain was drawn tight, trying to hide what lay just beyond. It was doing a poor job. The smallest of cracks in the material allowed my wandering eyes to steal a look inside. Instead of the usual lone nurse, he had two. I knew something wasn't right. Those helpful machines, the ones sustaining it all, were gone, the beeping silent. I kept looking. Perhaps he had been transferred, moved to a different room, maybe even discharged. My eyes scanned the bed, the only thing left in his room. A form lay there still and unmoving. Nothing abnormal there. The difference was the sheet, white, clean and pulled a different way today. It completely covered him head to foot. My heart clenched tight, and my mouth began sprouting cotton thick and full. I tried to swallow the growing crop down, but it was shooting up faster than the menacing weeds I yanked at in our garden. I was struggling. The nurses, somber and quiet, cleaned the last of the supplies and room with efficiency.

I reached Graham just in time, the nauseous feeling so overwhelming I was afraid I'd lose my breakfast. The small amount I'd consumed would still cause a scene if I couldn't make it somewhere safe.

Graham was propped in his chair which forced him to sit back slightly from its position. He had never been one to recline in any type of chair, being too busy for that kind of lifestyle. Sitting still for long periods of time where you could enjoy their comforts, relaxing in front of the television and even falling asleep, was not my Graham. His eyes were open a little more than the day before. Still, they were pathetic, unable to move, blink or focus on anything.

I hitched up my emotions forcing my true feelings elsewhere and placed a smile to my lips. There was no way he'd be seeing it anyway. And even if he could, he'd know it was fake.

"Hi Graham." I said it quietly into his ear, giving him a kiss and tender touch to his forehead and face. I had missed him. I missed him still, even though he was right there with me. I didn't know it yet but that day would be the beginning of the 'new Graham.' The new husband. The new father and son and brother and friend. He'd be a new man, different in so many ways. There'd be no going back to that first guy I knew. Learning to grieve him and all he had been would be the most bizarre thing I'd have to do.

He reacted to my greeting just as he had been doing for days now. Nothing. No movements. No eye contact. Nothing to let me know he was aware of my presence. But something made me look closer at him. Something *was* different today. I could feel it. It wasn't a reaction, a flash or even a spark. Whatever it was crossed his demeanor for only a fraction of a second. Was it my voice? My smell? Somehow, he *knew* I was here. He just did. But as fast as I felt it, it left. I looked around the room; surely his family sensed it too? No, their expressions were the same they had been. Sad and discouraged he was still like this. Maybe it was all in my head. Something not really there. I so desperately wanted to see something from him, some kind of sign; I'd do almost anything. I shook my head to clear my thoughts, filter my emotions. No. I hadn't made this up. Something had been there, even if only a passing feeling between husband and wife.

"Hi buddy!" Rick grabbed at his limp, unbound left hand and tried to pump a handshake out of it. There was no returned grip. Graham enjoyed hard handshakes, his fingers always wrapping solid and hard, pumping and moving to the ancient old greeting. I knew if he could see this shake between the brothers, he'd be disappointed with his performance.

Sarah sank into a chair by the wall. I watched her eyes pool with tears. This was a hard sight for her take in. A once strong and healthy brother unable to even hold his head up. She was only a few years older than Graham, with kids and a husband of her own. She had lost the same mother Graham had. And I knew the last thing she wanted was to go through another loss like that.

"Ok, you ready?" The nurse was looking right at me, waiting. I had forgotten all about her and her excitement.

"Yes, of course." I wasn't sure what to expect.

She untied his right arm from the rail; instantly the limb began flailing and sputtering like a fish in the bottom of a Johnboat.

"I went to hand him a tissue today to see what he'd do. I thought maybe he'd wipe his nose or something." She turned and pulled a single tissue from its box sitting near the sink.

"GRAHAM!" She yelled.

For someone so small, she could make quite the sound. Unprepared for it, I jumped with my own response.

"DO YOU WANT TO WIPE YOUR FACE?" What was it with everyone yelling at him?

Sarah leaned forward in her chair. Rick stood frozen in place next to me; all eyes fixed on the patient, on what he would do. I was skeptical. What *could* he do?

He couldn't find the tissue of course, but with her help he grabbed it fast and attempted to move it toward his face. He was almost there, maybe six inches from his forehead when he stopped, his hand sure it found what it needed. Instead, it wiped at only air. He methodically swiped back and forth at the space between his head and the white tissue. He made quick work of it, balling the paper into his hand like he was annoyed with the job. It went flying a few feet in front of him, sailing to the floor. It landed nowhere near the wastebasket.

"Isn't that great?" The nurse reached for another tissue and went about finishing the job he had tried to do. She wiped the sweat that had formed on his face from the small amount of exertion. She then tied his arm down again. It went without a fight.

"The Doctor's have already been in today and they agree, he's ready for some rehab." She was beaming ear to ear.

I wasn't sure what to do. Should I jump for joy? Cry with excitement? Or was that fear I was feeling? Fear of the unknown and being left with a husband whose only ability was to swipe at air with a tissue? I felt overwhelmed. And guilty. For the first time, my heart wondered if his life would be worth living. I was afraid to admit that if this was all I'd get back, he and I both would be happier if he was dead.

"That's so exciting." I lied and placed another fake smile to my face.

"We're just waiting for a room to open up over there."

"Over where?" I couldn't help but ask.

"Oh. Sunnyview Rehabilitation Hospital. It's not far from here. They specialize in things like this."

Things like this. There it was again. Something to remind me that we now had two heads. A forked tongue. A reminder we weren't normal anymore. I swallowed hard.

I had no idea what lay ahead. My strides were sick of taking it all in. But I hadn't a choice. It had to be better than staying here another minute longer. Better than being that boy's parent's left to bury their son. Maybe their only one. I was sick of watching people on the brink of death.

Yes, I had much to be thankful for. Graham was still here with me. Obviously fighting for his life. I was going to have to fight with him. For him. Whatever the outcome and however he healed. I was going to have to step out of my role as his wife and into a role I had never been before. His coach. His trainer. Oftentimes, his mother. My journey was about to be kicked up a whole other notch.

For Graham, that man of mine lying with the blank stare, hurting mind and bruised body was about to begin the ride of his life. The most difficult yet. One he hadn't realized he'd signed up for. The terrain would be intense, the stakes high. His once rock-solid faith would be put through test after test, and he'd be forced to face the most difficult of obstacles. While I had been dealing with this for weeks, he was just getting started. Still, I knew if anyone was wired for this, it was Graham. His mind may have been mixed up and disoriented. But his soul wasn't jumbled, muddled or confused. No. That piece of him would be impossible to be plucked, ridiculous to be pulled and hopeless to be torn from where it sat—tucked neatly in the strongest of Palms. Safe and sound.

13
HE'S IN THERE

*'God creates out of nothing. Wonderful you say. Yes, to be sure, but
He does what is still more wonderful: He makes saints out of sinners.'*
~Soren Kierkegaard

I was there when they loaded him in the first time. The ambulance exactly how you see it in the movies, the American ones anyway: white, red, some lettering on the sides and front, the stainless steel floor so clean could you eat off it. He had been unconscious then, dirt-covered and broken, his future shaky and unknown. Now, almost 4 weeks later his future was still shaky. But at least he was alive.

I missed that second ride, the one taking him from his small ICU room to a nearby rehabilitation hospital. I would never forget that room and all it had done to me. Or that floor and all I had witnessed. I'd miss a few of the nurse's who so painstakingly went above and beyond what was expected of them. But that was it.

They told me he went via wheelchair. Strapped and secured with no chance of breaking free. Not that he needed any restraining—other than that arm. It was hard to say where he was in his level of coma. Conscious? Semi-conscious? Neither? I was learning these comas were as unique and different as our own fingerprints or the snowflakes that so often pounded our home. Every one unlike the next.

I could almost see the ramp lowering, allowing him to be wheeled up and inside, the wheels locking into place. His eyes were probably huge like the deer are when your headlights hit them straight on in the middle of a dark road. Or perhaps they were closed in sleep. That's how he was most of the time anyway. He hadn't been outside since the accident. Could he sense the changes around him? The sun hot in his face, its bright rays maybe making him sweat or squint. Had he missed it?

I hoped someone held his hand; that he wasn't left in the back of that ambulance alone like a caged dog.

I was home packing his stuff for the new place. Sneakers. Some clothes. A toothbrush. I jammed his old snowboarding bag much too full, his dresser drawers creaking at my constant yanking and pulling to find the perfect items. I hadn't been in these drawers in over 3 weeks. There had been no reason to. The endless laundry he usually produced had quickly come to a standstill. Yet everything was just as he had left it. The top one holding socks, some underwear and that handgun, the one he had gotten only a few months before. We knew the top drawer was no original hiding place for a gun, but the pistol still burrowed itself nicely under the garments in a small black case. It just fit there. He had been so excited to get that silly thing. I wondered if he'd ever be able to shoot it again. I pushed it aside to find more pocketknives, belt buckles and a few other miscellaneous things. I headed for his toothbrush in the bathroom. There it sat, the bristles hard and stiff from sitting far too long without any use. I stuffed it on top of some shirts and zipped the bag shut.

Today would be the day. The start of those first therapy sessions. Whatever that meant. I guessed it to mean the first day of getting him back to his old self. Or at the very least trying to. I rounded the corner to his new room with a mix of anxiousness and excitement. This place was different. Maybe a bit homier and not as depressing. Some of the patients actually appeared normal as they walked the halls or sat in their wheelchairs and ate the tray of food in front of them. Still others didn't fair as well. Propped in wheelchairs or beds, their bodies looked tight and uncomfortable. Some were twisted and cocked in a way that seemed painful. Most were older, apparent stroke victims. But there were others too. A few young adults and even some children. So small. So helpless. My heart swelled with pain at seeing their little bodies tremble and convulse from their injuries, the messages from brain to body obviously muddled with clutter.

It was here we found ourselves, the floor with all the other TBI and stroke patients. I wandered around until I found the secretaries desk. I couldn't get his room number fast enough, my eyes scanning the doorframes for the correct one. My feet naturally followed while I passed room after room, the numbers climbing. I had to be getting close. There it was. Room 376.

A wheelchair in the middle of the hallway caught my attention. I had to do a double take. It was Graham. He was out of that saggy hospital gown and dressed in some borrowed shorts and shirt. It didn't fit him well but at this point anything would've looked better than the sack I got used to seeing.

He sat suspended in one of those high-tech wheelchairs complete with a head support, four wheels instead of two, feet rests and an anti-tip function. I would learn later this would keep him from tipping himself backwards possibly causing more damage.

He was staring right at me and my heart skipped a beat. I looked closer. No. He wasn't seeing me, not by a long shot. He was lost with eyes opened too widely with no light behind them. Instead of that right hand being restrained and unable to move, it now donned a white mit much like a boxing glove. He'd be doing no such sport any time soon. The glove velcroed in place with two straps stretching across the backside, any normal functioning person would've been able to undo it easily. Even a small child. But not Graham. He moved his new gear all around and I wondered if he'd stopped since the last time I saw him.

His now thin legs wore tall circulation socks up to his knees with both legs shaking violently. I instantly thought the worst. A Seizure. Or something more. I was about to panic when I looked up and saw her for the first time.

"That shaking he's doing is actually very normal for right now." A girl much my age bent over the side of Graham's wheelchair, grabbed each leg and carefully began stretching them out. She went on explaining, trying to put my mind at ease.

"He's lost so much muscle tone his legs don't know what to do with themselves." She ended by flexing the ball of his foot and returned them to their place. The bouncing didn't stop completely, but it was better. Happy with her results she went and stood behind Graham, hands on his shoulders in an almost protective mode. Her eyes locked in on mine.

"Hi" She said finally, her face warm. Our hands greeted with Graham plopped in the middle of it all.

"Hello" I wasn't sure about this girl who was hovering over my husband. She obviously worked here and had claimed Graham as her own. I didn't know what to say next. Good thing she did.

"I'm going to be Graham's physical therapist while he's here." Her hair swayed slightly while she talked. It made me look closer. Long and beautiful, some of the strands pulled themselves back into a cute fashion fitting her exactly. I subconsciously grabbed at my own hair. My decision to hack my own long locks just a couple days ago was quickly beginning to become a regret.

My eyes continued to look at her. Her face was smooth and soft with large brown eyes staring quietly and confidently back at me. It didn't take long for me to notice her secret. Her blessing actually. She wasn't going to be able to keep this hidden much longer. That swell had started, the one of her unborn baby. I almost missed it hiding behind the chair so easily. It'd be another couple months before she'd be uncomfortable, that she wouldn't fit so nicely behind and beside things. But for right now she was still herself. Still able to move freely and easily, like even she forgot she had this life inside her, growing and maturing each day.

My mind spun. This wasn't what I had prepared for. I had pictured more of the drill sergeant type to be standing here. A *man* ready to whip Graham back into shape, pushing him to make him what he once was. Not this girl, pregnant and probably younger than me. I waited for her to speak.

"You must be Graham's wife?" I could tell she was sincere.

"Yes, I am." I almost hated admitting this. Not out of shame. I was simply weary from all the bad news. My heart braced for more of it, stacking another brick of protection around my growing fortified wall. I knew there were never going to be enough bricks.

"I'm Fallon." My eyes went to the nametag clipped to her shirt. Her name was unique. Pretty. Like her.

"I just finished my evaluation of him and I'd like to talk to you about him." I noticed her clipboard for the first time. It sat casually in her arms.

What was penned there?

"Do you have a minute?" Graham's legs were beginning to shake again, but she remained focused on me. I wasn't sure I wanted to hear what she'd have to say. But it looked like I hadn't a choice.

"Okay." I said.

She had to know I was tired. She had to know I had been drug through the wringer these last weeks. I hoped she'd go easy on me.

She glanced a moment at her notes, but I could tell she didn't really need to. She already knew what she was going to say.

"He's in there." Her eyes were trying to read my blank expression, like I should know what she meant by this simple statement.

"Ex-excuse me?" I stammered, unsure.

"He's in there." She went on.

"He's very consistent with a frontal lobe brain injury, but from the looks of it, he's showing me great signs of recovering from this."

"How can you tell?" I looked at Graham like I was seeing him for the first time. Maybe I was missing something.

"The signs are extremely small still. It's true he's been hurt very badly."

There it was. I knew it couldn't *all* be good news.

"However, he *is* doing something good for me, his eyes being the biggest encouragement." I leaned down to look into Graham's eyes. I wanted to see what she was seeing. But they looked the same as they always had since this all started. What was I missing?

"Even though they appear like they're looking at nothing he will occasionally track a few people that come into his room." It was hard for her to hide the excitement she had, her hands moving as fast as Graham's bouncy legs and mitted hand.

I found myself smiling back at her. A real smile, not the fake kind I had gotten so good at putting on. She wasn't done.

"He can totally hear you right now too."

"He can?" I looked at Graham in disbelief.

"He most definitely can. He knows you're here right now, he just won't remember it, so try to act as normal as possible with him. It'll help him heal faster."

"Okay." I grabbed his crazy hand and tried to quiet it.

She watched us a moment, my happy tears threatening to spill over.

"This is going to be a long road for him. And for you. But I'm hopeful he'll be functional again one day." She touched my arm gently. She would never know how much I needed to hear something like this. Something positive about Graham and his condition.

"The encouragement and stability he receives from you will be vital in his recovery process." I stood back up slowly to look her square on. I didn't need to read between any lines. I knew what she was telling me I had to do.

Someone was going to have to be strong, able to help and do whatever it took to make him feel comfortable in his new skin. His new brain. Someone was going to have to put emotions elsewhere, step up to the plate to get the job done. That someone was me—the coach, encourager, teacher and trainer. I'd still be his wife, his best friend, his favorite. But for right now all that was going to have to wait for another time. Another day.

"I must be going, but I have a session with him soon if you want to observe it. I'll stop back later to pick him up. You can tag along wherever we go." She turned to leave.

"Hang in there." She said compassionately. She stopped short and looked at Graham.

"GRAHAM, I'LL SEE YOU SOON!" She headed down the hall.

I didn't know it yet, but this young girl, this young therapist; the one I completely underestimated would become pivotal in not just Graham's life, but mine as well. She had been specially picked. Somehow. Someway, it was meant to be. Her belief in Graham and all he could be would become the driving force, the thing to make her push and fight to get what she wanted out of him. Her youth would only add fuel to her fire of unique methods and techniques.

I watched her disappear into another room to another patient with loved ones waiting.

I grabbed at the wheelchair and attempted to move it into his room. I wanted to see where he'd be staying. Where he'd sleep and lie and sit. I began walking but the chair remained planted in place not budging an inch. My momentum caused the back of Graham's headrest to hit my stomach. I looked around, certain someone would be smirking at me. I fumbled around looking for a release button. I had so much to learn. So much to understand in this world of caring for your completely disabled loved one. It was going to be the hardest thing I had ever done before. Still, I was willing, still that young horse working hard at the task at hand. I had no choice. The Dark Stretch remained my path. My course. And I was going to finish.

I waited awkwardly until a nurse taught me Wheelchair Driving 101. We were soon off, sailing smoothly into his room and new life awaiting us. I only bumped into the doorframe once.

14
ANGEL'S LANDING

'Every day you may make progress. Every step may be fruitful. Yet there will stretch out before you an ever-lengthening, ever-ascending, ever-improving path. You know you will never get to the end of the journey. But this, so far from discouraging, only adds to the joy and glory of the climb.'
~Winston Churchill

I had to look away. A small child strapped to a bench-like seat was being worked on. She was almost vertical in an angle she had no control over. Pieces of equipment wrapped themselves around her chest like a snake coiled in a death-like vice. But this didn't want to kill; rather it jiggled and shook the small body gently trying to restore life, not take it. I guessed this to mean it was loosening the secretions in the chest, her own too frail to dislodge anything itself. I was right.

Arms draped this way and that, her legs bending and forming not quite right. A ventilator stood breathing for her like the consistent workhorse it was. In and out. In and out. There was so much equipment required for someone this size. Too much equipment. I would never learn what her story was.

"You can have a seat right over there." Fallon steered Graham toward a padded and raised area. We were in the 'gym'. Not quite the kind you grow up in, running laps and throwing dodge balls. There were only a few things I was familiar with. The floor was wooden and perfectly waxed like she was ready for a big game of basketball. But, she was too small, and no scuffmarks had ever traced her face. A few pieces of equipment at first glance looked ready for a hard workout though there were too many straps, too many extra pieces meant for added support for those disabled. Those like my Graham. I continued walking the open floor plan passing many other patients and their accompanying therapists.

The back wall sported 3-4 of these raised bench-like beds. We headed for the third one. A few patients in the open area practiced walking and standing. Some even balanced on those big workout balls reaching with all their might for a cone, bean bag or other item on the outer brink of their grasp. Out of all the things in the room, those balls were the most recognizable to me. They had come in handy when I labored, enduring those seemingly never-ending birthing pains.

Most here were like Graham. Wheelchair bound. Unable to do anything themselves. These patients sat or lay on padded benches, completely supported by assistants and therapists. Their legs were stretched and worked gently back and forth. Again and again. Some were trying to do it themselves, following the commands given them. Others needed help, their limbs too uncoordinated, their heads too heavy to hold up on their own. They drooped and hung like newborn babies do.

I realized I hadn't taken a breath since I entered this room. I was too uncomfortable. A feeling of guilt was hovering over my heart. *My* own legs had carried me here. *My* arms swung and hung like they should with smooth movements. *My* eyes focused and unfocused on things I didn't even know about. And this all happened in the time it took to walk these few short steps. It was much more than anyone here could do. But it had been so simple for me. Thoughtless. Easy.

My whole perspective on life had changed weeks before. My attitude and outlook more sensitive, more loving. And now, in this room, where time literally stood still, I'd begin to see all I truly had to be thankful for. Even now. Even with Graham as he was.

"GRAHAM, WE'RE GOING TO MOVE YOU TO THIS MAT. DO YOU THINK YOU COULD GIVE US A HAND?"

I almost laughed out loud. Was she serious? He was sleeping in his chair, his head completely supported and unable to move. I plopped down where she told me to and waited for the scene to unfold into something more. I had no idea what to expect.

A man appeared out of the corner of my eye. Strong. Able. Experienced. In one easy movement, he lifted Graham from the wheelchair and sat him carefully on the mat. He held him secure while Fallon adjusted all the tubing that had traveled the distance from chair to mat. There was the IV tube with its stand on wheels, the stomach tube poking its way out from under his shirt and the blood pressure cuff inflating and deflating every few minutes. His back and neck braces needed a quick twist to set back correctly and the trache in his neck bobbled up and down much like an Adam's apple.

Graham had helped in no way at all. If he only knew another man had just picked him up like the rag-doll he was, he'd be madder than a hornet. The man completely supported him, holding his upper body and head where it should be. Wobbly legs dangled over the edge in a most awkward way, barely touching the ground. Sweat beaded and formed on his face, pouring and dripping like a leaky faucet.

"Believe it or not, he's working really hard right now. And this sweating he's doing is normal." Fallon reached for a folded towel nearby and attempted to wipe at Graham's face, neck and arms.

"GRAHAM, I'M NOT SURE I'VE EVER HAD SOMEONE SWEAT THIS BAD!" She laughed, continuing to wipe, completely fixated on Graham and his needs. She had forgotten everyone else in the room and after an okay blood pressure reading and temperature take, she sank onto a stool in front of Graham and continued.

"I'M GOING TO ASK YOU A FEW QUESTIONS AND YOU NEED TO TRY TO RESPOND SO WE CAN COMMUNICATE TOGETHER OKAY?"

His eyes had opened some in the move and his legs bounced uncontrollably.

"CAN YOU GIVE ME A THUMBS UP IF YOU'RE IN PAIN?"

My eyes went to his hands. Limp. Motionless. Could he really be paying attention right now?

Nothing happened.

"HOW BOUT JUST A THUMBS UP?"

Again. Nothing. My heart sank in disappointment.

"ALRIGHT GRAHAM, THAT'S OKAY. MAYBE YOU DON'T LIKE TO GIVE THUMBS UP. LET'S TRY TO STICK OUT YOUR TONGUE. CAN YOU DO THAT FOR ME? CAN YOU STICK OUT YOUR TONGUE GRAHAM?"

Fallon's face was so close, right in front of his, peering into the lost and trapped person he was, hoping he'd send out the slightest signal he was still in there.

Only a few moments passed, but it felt like forever. I was about to look away, too disturbed to keep watching, when it happened. There it was. The smallest part of his tongue, the tip, slowly stuck its way out. It went back in even more slowly, his face unchanged, his eyes empty.

"GREAT JOB GRAHAM! WELL DONE." Fallon was smiling at him. I was too.

A huge mountain clearly loomed in front of Graham. In front of us both. And it was bigger than any of the ones in the Adirondacks. This was more like the ones you see out West, jagged, straight up and near impossible to conquer. Yet, people do. All the time. With patience and willpower and endurance, we were going to have to climb this. Our trek something we'd *have* to get done. Conquer. We simply didn't have a choice.

I wouldn't consider us experienced hikers when we set out years ago to hike the famous 'Angel's Landing' in Zion National Park, part of Utah's best. We were young, without kids and on the vacation of a lifetime. Still, we felt ready and excited for the magnificent view.

The paved path was more than we were used to, and I smiled at the memories of many other hiking adventures back home. Getting lost and searching for those trail markers like they were golden nuggets happened more times than I'd like to admit. This should be easy. A walk in the park. A quick trip up.

What I hadn't taken into account was the narrow rocky pass. Like a dizzying and spiny vertebrae of some sort of enormous mystical creature, it twisted and turned its way to the top. The edges dropped off just feet away from my hiking boots. I felt certain my number was up.

It didn't take long for me to freeze with fear. The nice paved path had vanished, replacing itself with huge chain links drilled into the steep face of a cliff. They were supposed to support me, balance me in place until I reached the top. But, I wasn't so sure. The terrain was hard and rocky, so I should've been able to handle this.

It was the heights that were getting to me. I had never been a fan, my fear outweighing any kind of logical thinking. The rush of adrenaline never worth it for me. My legs quickly turned to Jell-O, shaky and unable to hold me. I was forced to sit, my arms wrapping tightly to a chain, the edge much too close for my comfort. I now understood why it held the name 'Angel's Landing'. This had to be the closest place to them for me. Graham looked back at me, his smile beaming with excitement. This was right up his ally. And we were almost there. Almost to the top.

I knew my face said it all, and he was by my side in a heartbeat.

"You can do this."

I was too afraid to talk, the edge right there, my mind reeling with the thought of falling. Just one misstep, and I'd be done. My life over. My whole body was trembling, my wobbly feet unable to find a proper foothold. I knew it was all in my head. That if I could just get control of this fear, I'd be able to do it.

If the trail had allowed for him to carry me, Graham would've. But there was no other way. I'd have to take myself. From where I sat, I didn't want to go up. And I didn't want to go down either. The thought of continuing either way was too overwhelming. I was stuck. Stranded. Thoughts turned to us staying here for the night and if we could survive it. How long would it take for a rescue team to come get me? I was becoming irrational, my panic button pushed again and again by my fear.

"RANDI!" My eyes slowly re-focused. Graham was yelling at me.

"I can try to help you. But, *YOU* have to do this." He was gripping my ankles, squatting in a way that if I did fall, he'd be coming with me. He didn't usually talk to me this firmly. I had become like a child to him. His child.

I slowly stood. My surroundings already my worst nightmare. I took a step, Graham's hand there to guide my distressed foot into a secure hold. If he was scared, he wasn't letting me see it. He had to know it wouldn't help my cause. I took another. And another. Each step slow and heavy. Nothing inside me wanted to continue.

But we did.

And now, it was my turn to be the strong one. The one unafraid. The one placing his feet where they'd need to be so we could get to the top. I couldn't show my fear. I couldn't let him see what was really going on inside my head. My heart.

He had done well today, following a simple command given him. Granted, it was slow, me almost missing it with my untrained eye. Still, it said so much. While he remained trapped and caught in a place where escape seemed impossible, he was trying to get out. He wanted out. He didn't want to stay where he was. Somehow he was going to climb and fight his way up out of the valley where he was now held prisoner. We'd do it together. I just knew it.

15
"YOU'RE SMOKIN' HOT"

'God will not look you over for medals, degrees or diplomas but for scars.'

~Elbert Hubbard

Sitting in a car for three hours a day traveling back and forth from the hospital gave me lots of time to think. And pray. This period of time was just long enough to help me gear up for the day, and also unwind at the end. I was the one sitting behind the steering wheel, my foot on the pedal, my seat belt clicked into place, but it wasn't *really* me. Getting to my destination each day was a feat for the army of angels that had to guide my white mini-van as we wound our way down the Northway and into the hospital parking lot. I knew this because oftentimes, my vision was blurred with tears, my hands too shaky to really hold tight, and my mind anywhere but on the road. I wasn't used to driving in traffic, the cars much too close and aggressive than I liked. But it was do or die. Keep up or get run off the road. So I learned quickly.

The constant therapy was draining, and I was exhausted both physically and emotionally by the time I left Graham each evening. Just weeks before I had been instructing in the heat, riding horses and managing a crew of wranglers. But there was no comparison; this was harder. I sat. I pushed him around. I talked to him. I watched and encouraged. I helped in his therapies by holding or handing cones, blocks or balls to him. By the end of the day, I was thankful his parents were staying in a nearby motel offering relief and comfort to me when I couldn't take it any longer.

I liked to arrive by 8:30 every morning, just in time for his first session. He did better when I was around. At least I liked to think he did. He was always in the same spot by the window in his room overlooking the parking lot, strapped into his chair. I never liked to disturb him. His back to me, his head now able to support itself; he looked almost normal. But he was far from it. His mitted hand became more agitated by the hour, rubbing and touching the oddest of places on his body. The bridge of his nose was completely raw and bloody from it, and I was constantly pulling at his wrist, trying to comfort and relax it. He was obsessed with it.

Today his demeanor was different, his eyes moving more than I'd seen them move in a long time, darting back and forth like he was trying to focus on something. The only problem: he couldn't. I watched him a moment. He was trying to tell me something. I knew it.

"What can I get you?" His hand was reaching and grabbing for me. I couldn't resist, my head coming close to his face. He amazed me at how strong he still was. For a moment I couldn't break free, he was pulling me in by my neck. Maybe he wanted a hug. Or maybe he was just happy to see me today. But he was hurting me. His grip strong and unrelenting. There was nothing gentle and loving about this embrace.

I had to work hard to get free, taking a step back and holding my neck where a red mark was sure to appear. He had never done this before, and I knew something was wrong. But what?

He continued his tirade a moment longer, his limitations preventing him from communicating normally. He couldn't get anything out. He was still unable to talk. Unable to move other than that arm. And those bouncy legs. Both were in overdrive, and all I could do was stand there and watch him struggle.

He was sweating again like he had just finished the hardest therapy yet. Maybe he was tired. Maybe he was over-stimulated. Maybe it was something more. But, there I was with only my guesses, like that student afraid to circle the answer, certain to make a mistake. I went for the sink, a wet paper towel would at least wipe the sweat, ease some of the heat. I turned back, ready to wipe and dry his face and finally saw what all the fuss was about.

His gray sweatpants, ones we bought for him so he'd be more comfortable, were soaked through, a darker gray wetting most of the material. Now relaxed and at ease, he sat still, even his arm resting quietly by his side. I felt awful. But also, oddly happy. He'd been trying to communicate with me. His need to use the bathroom was something he was aware of, something he knew he needed. It was huge.

I ran for a nurse. She'd know what to do.

"Well, we're going to have to transfer him back to the bed so we can change him." She said this after quickly assessing the situation and rolling his chair next to the bed.

"You should probably learn how to do this anyway. Come over here and give me a hand."

Only a few days here had made me see how much work taking care of a grown man truly was. A grown disabled man. Nothing was easy. Or fast. He was like a big infant complete with diapers, formula type-food, completely dependent on those around him. I knew the staff worked hard to take care of him. Change him. Move him. Dress him. But it hadn't been my turn yet. I hadn't been asked. I hadn't been trained. Apparently now, it was time.

How hard could it be? I changed diapers all the time. My kids produced more than their fair share of dirty wipes. I had even done the whole cloth diaper thing with them, making the whole experience even more challenging. I pulled my short hair back with the elastic I kept on my arm like this would somehow help the situation. I helped her get Graham to the edge of the bed. The nurse and I grunted and yanked, and he finally made it to the center, the bed rails lowered and out of the way.

"You're going to want those." She nodded to the sink directly behind me. I turned searching for what she could be talking about. It took me a couple seconds. I fished out two bright blue medical gloves and snapped them over my fingers. I stood staring at my raised hands a moment much like the Doctors must once they've washed and prepped themselves for surgery. I was ready to push open that door with my body, hands clear of bacteria and germs. I could do this. There was nothing to it.

"First, you'll have to undress his lower body." She nodded to his shoes, his pants.

I set right to work, stripping his shoes, his wet pants and undoing the diaper that hadn't done a very good job of keeping him dry. It took me a bit longer than it did my children, but I did it. I tossed the sweats into the corner and the diaper into the trash. So far so good.

The nurse instructed me with the new diaper, the folded plastic, cotton, and tape to hold it all in place opening like a fan, a newspaper. I knew now why it had done such a poor job of keeping him dry. The awkward piece reminded me of the hospital gown he had worn in the ICU, saggy, unflattering and much too big for my now 170 pound husband.

Graham slept on, completely unaware that his wife was taking care of him in this way. He was such a man's man. This was going to be humbling for him. Fortunately, he wouldn't remember. Besides, I didn't mind. Truly, I didn't. I loved him and if this was what I had to do, I was going to do it and not complain. I was going to serve him if needed like this until the end. I took a big breath and continued on.

I had to roll him on his side to position the diaper just right. That was the easy part. He rolled easily back, the diaper hidden somewhere underneath him. I reached for one of his legs. It was more like lifting a huge tree branch, the kind my dad was always cutting down in our yard, us kids dragging them to the edge of the field to burn. This was tricky and so unlike the babies I was used to. Their little legs I could hold in one hand; lift up and get the job done in no time. The nurse grabbed the other one, blue gloves now lining her hands as well. Before long we were done with fresh clothes back on his body. I didn't quite understand him needing the shoes, but they were adamant he wear them. I tied them and placed them back on the feet rests of his wheelchair.

We were once again left staring out the window, the parking lot the only thing to look at with a few people milling around searching for their cars, cups of hot coffee in their hands. Here, in the quiet of his room, I determined to pay better attention to his needs. He was sitting up for now, his eyes quickly becoming too heavy to keep open. He'd be out soon, so peaceful, not a care in the world. I watched him drift realizing his communication wasn't what it once was. Far from it. But, he was trying.

Like learning a new language, studying, perfecting, so I'd now have to do with him. I'd have to get it down better than I had done in my Spanish classes in high school. My observations of him and his needs were critical. My love for him was stronger than anyone else. Because of this love, I'd have to fight for his comfort and the words he couldn't get out. His life.

I must've done a good job changing him, passing some imaginary test, because I was soon learning other things to help Graham throughout the day. And most surprisingly, he learned them too. I helped him brush his teeth, the occupational therapist even allowing him to give it a try. He missed his mouth, brushing at air, but he got better as each day passed. He was soon doing it himself, following the commands given to him. I shaved his stubbly face, the trache in his neck plugged, but still very much there and a difficult thing to get around with a razor. I slowly managed.

The speech therapist introduced ice chips, his chewing and swallowing a bit scary at first. He quickly mastered it, and she added thickened water and juice to his diet. I learned the working of throat and mouth, the chewing and swallowing oftentimes opened a whole new door for those like Graham in their progression and healing. And it did just that for him.

Noise began forming deep in his throat. Grunting and moaning, growling and rumbling. The noises babies often make worked their way up and out very slowly. He wasn't talking yet, but he was getting close. I couldn't wait to hear what I hadn't in so long—his words, his voice.

When handed a pencil, we learned Graham could still write. He could do his numbers, his address, the days of the week. His ability to follow commands began improving, and I looked forward to seeing him each day and all the new things he could do.

Physically he began improving too. His right hand, the one with the mit began to calm down. It was like he realized it to be that unruly child needing discipline and structure, and he started using its abilities for positive things. He was even allowed to go without the nuisance for periods of chaperoned time. He worked hard to stretch and reach and move all his limbs. They were a bit tense, sometimes jerky. But, he persisted on. His left arm gave him the most trouble. It liked to stay tucked against his chest, its tightness at times painful and frustrating for him. It was obvious he was going to have the most challenge with that arm, those fingers.

Almost overnight the growling turned into whispering and after many weeks of silence my prayers were answered. Graham began saying things.

"He said thank you to me this morning while I changed him." It was his nurse, and her eyes told me of her genuine happiness at his progress.

I couldn't wait to hear it myself but walked slowly to him, not wanting to startle him. He knew who I was now, and I was thankful we wouldn't have to overcome that obstacle as well.

"Hi Graham." I bent to give him a kiss on his cheek. His eyes moved to my face. Recognition was there, and I waited for something to come out, anything to let me know he was in there. His whispers reached my ears, but I had to lean close to make it out. He was so quiet.

He said it again, and this time there was no mistake.

"You're smokin' hot!" I heard him loud and clear and laughed at his remark, his own smile reached his lips, crooked and wobbly, but there. It was the first I had seen in a long time.

I was thrilled. Graham was coming out of that dark dungeon he was in. He was climbing higher to the summit, the beautiful view soon to be seen. A full recovery right over the next knoll. But it was going to be some time to see the tree line where the light peers faintly through, where the brush is thinner, the air lighter.

"I want a divorce. You need to divorce me." He said this just ten minutes after his first comment, my smile, my predictions, my dreams, quickly fading. His words became an unfiltered and confused mess. I had to come to grips that while it was good he was talking, his speech beginning to form like it once did, he didn't always play nice.

Graham had never talked to me or anyone else with disrespect. I was forced to roll with whatever came tumbling out next, my laughter always the best medicine for us both. His knew found voice proved what we all feared. He didn't know what had happened to him, how he got here, or where he was going. He was sure he had been in a car accident, a boating accident. His answers changed each time he was asked. But they were never one involving his horse, his Crockett. He didn't think it possible.

Each time he was asked to name the day, time, month or even year, he got it wrong. Some days he was in 1999. Other times he was sure he got his hamburgers from Jerusalem and that his dead mother was still alive. I could almost see his brain with all the fuses cut short, spinning to find a connection to something. Anything.

We'd remain on a roller coaster of Graham's high highs and low lows for some time. He'd be antsy and frustrated, or sedate and lethargic, laughing uncontrollably, or weeping like I'd never seen him weep. Still, I never walked away from him. I continued on, pushing him, potty-training him, tying his shoes, and massaging his legs and arms. I cleaned his ears, applied lotion to his unused feet, and clipped his terribly long fingernails and toenails. I did all this while talking to him, sharing with him, trying to connect with him. But I knew. Deep down I knew he wouldn't remember a thing of it. His ability to live beyond the present was impossible for him. He reminded me of our dogs. No thought of the future and uncaring for the past.

It was a lonely time for me. I had my husband. Yet, I didn't.

Fallon persisted on with Graham, pulling him from his wheelchair and forcing him into all kinds of positions. She pushed him harder than anyone else there, and it was just what he needed. She rotated him, stretched him, stood him up and sat with him. It was a big day when he could finally sit up on his own without someone supporting him. He was proud of himself, his smile only showing on half his face. The right side. The other side drooped and hung like the floppy ears of a bloodhound.

Soon, it'd be time. Time for him to learn how to walk once again.

I wandered in front, acting like a carrot facing the horse, a dangling temptation to follow. Two others completely supported Graham on each side, a safety belt strapped to his midsection. Ace bandages wove their way up and around his feet and calves holding the balls of his feet bent and curled. They were so limp and uncoordinated he couldn't pick them up to form a normal step. I was sure they were crazy, that this was never going to work.

But I did as they asked, talking and tempting Graham to follow me, my voice a welcoming sound to his ears. Those first few steps were agonizing to witness. He seemed to be helping in no way at all, his weight completely suspended by the pregnant Fallon and her poor assistant for the day. They were the ones moving and placing each leg and foot exactly where it needed to be. Not Graham.

Sweaty and done for the day, only a few feet covered, Graham sank into his chair. His eyes quickly closed in deep sleep. Fallon's own sweat beaded on her forehead. I was completely discouraged.

"He did great!" She looked at me, her smile huge.

"Really? I thought that looked awful." I was comfortable enough with her now to let her know exactly how I felt. I was certain she was just trying to make me feel better.

"Really, that was a good first time. He'll get it." She recorded his work down in a notebook, her smile still evident, the sweat just beginning to dry on her forehead.

Fallon wasn't discouraged. She knew Graham. She knew how to push, back off or continue on with his therapy. Each day she walked Graham a bit longer, a bit farther down the hall, and each day he got a little better, a little more balanced and sure. He wasn't ready to do it alone, but he was making headway.

His trache was finally removed leaving a hole in his neck that had to heal on its own. It was a strange thing to look at, like a red cherry, bright and out of place. The final piece to go was that feeding tube. The one keeping him alive, nourishing him. I was happy to say goodbye to it. A quick snip of some sutures and a deflated balloon inside his stomach sealed the deal. It slid out like the slippery noodle it was.

His ability to form complete thoughts, work through problems and solve them was fascinating to watch. His mind was there; no doubt about it. But the damage was great, his brain unsure how to find the words, the thoughts, the order to it all. Some days were great, his progress undeniable. Other days were discouraging, his habits and behavior hard to accept.

One habit was his love for counting. He'd count all day. Out loud. Non-stop. It didn't matter where we were or what we were doing, he had to be counting. By the end of the day, he was up into the thousands or higher. I was impressed and even started dreaming of numbers and counting them myself.

There was no doubt Graham was loved. He had become a character on his floor, his quick wit and odd sayings made everyone laugh. Every therapist, every nurse and every family member prodded him on. He was loved. Cherished. And we were all there for him. He sensed it too, his own affections showing a little more each day. He laughed with us. He cried with us. He knew there was something wrong with him. But he trusted me. He trusted us all. Even when he was confused and lost, he never forgot that I was somehow his, that his dad belonged by his side, and that his mom was someone he loved. Most importantly, he never forgot his Lord. He talked of Jesus and how he loved Him, how He had saved him all those years ago. He even liked telling the other patients about his King. It was sweet. It was a glimpse into the real Graham. A tender heart uncooked, raw.

After only six weeks in the rehabilitation hospital, talk of a visit home was marked on the calendar. The boys would finally get to see their dad, the one they still asked about, still missed. It had been a long 2 months for me. For us all. I couldn't wait.

16
THE SHIMMERING WILLOW

'What if you slept? And what if, in your sleep, you went to heaven and there plucked a strange and beautiful flower? And what if, when you awoke, you had the flower in your hand? Ah, what then?'
~Samuel Taylor Coleridge

He came on a Sunday afternoon, his wheelchair fitting nicely in his parent's car, folded and bent just right, the leg rests removed. It'd only be a few hours that I'd have him, but it was good enough for me. For us all. Our families were there; thrilled to be a part of what was happening today, what it all meant.

We were happy. We were thankful.

A day with the summer season past maturity signified to me much of what we'd been through: tried and true. The leaves sat thick on branches prepared and almost ready to make those magnificent colors pop and turn once again. They were always so faithful.

The grass was still green, but you could tell they were ready to call it a day to end all that growth. The blades had to be tired of the constant sound of the lawn mower, the rake picking up their loose ends. This changing over of seasons was always bittersweet for me. The adjustment hard, transition difficult. It's the moving out of the old to welcome in the new. Knowing things will never be the same and you'll never be able to go back. How you like it lies somewhere else. I knew it'd be the same for us.

I pushed Graham around our yard. Wyatt ran on ahead, not quite sure what to think of his father in the wheeled contraption, the restriction, the ruckus of it all. The back and neck braces threw him off a bit too, but his smile still met Graham's face occasionally. I knew with time, he'd be fine.

Keith sat on Graham's lap too young to care. He was happy just to be held and loved on, the ride a fun pastime. I couldn't yet tell if Graham truly knew his youngest son. The recognition of this little one hadn't really been there. Thankfully, Graham's sweet personality couldn't say no to a child. Any child, whether it was his or not.

I struggled to make it through the lumpy yard. I had become spoiled with all the carpeted hallways, tiled floors and paved walks at the hospital. My arms burned, the resistance, the strain, tempting me to give up. Maybe I should give someone else the job. I was embarrassed at how weak I had become. I headed for the barn, to the horses and garden area. I hoped the sights and sounds from this place would be music to his ears, art to his eyes.

He'd be walking soon, his balance improving daily. Pool therapy with Fallon was an added blessing. He was thriving in the water where those once bright noodles he bopped me over the head with, were now supporting and holding him, keeping him afloat, teaching him to walk. They had become a helpful tool, no longer a playful toy.

Still, he wasn't ready to do it alone and certainly couldn't be trusted. A few falls back at his room forced an aide to be with him at all times. That and an alarm-type bracelet strapped to his wrist and ankle. He was good at setting the sirens off when he decided to spin his chair out of bounds or leave the confines of it completely. He was his own worst enemy.

My mind was still reeling from the events earlier in the day. The drive, the family, the food, the visiting had all been too much for Graham. At least I thought so. He needed a good rest, his eyelids heavy and falling like the slow spill of molasses in wintertime. I'd have to stay with him but welcomed the thought of us resting together in our own bed. It had been far too long.

The mastering of transferring him from wheelchair to bed, or car, or anywhere else for that matter got him under the covers for some sleep. He wasn't completely helpless anymore. He assisted now even supporting most of his own weight. I slipped the sneakers off and placed them on the floor. That neck brace was in a ridiculous position, and I had to once again readjust and work it back where it belonged. I had never seen him hate something more. But, there was nothing he could do about it. Yanking at the uncomfortable plastic resulted in a scolding from me, from Fallon, from family and anyone else catching his prying hands. He was slowly learning to leave it alone.

I looked down at him; eyes shut, sleep right around the corner. He really was like a child in so many ways, and I couldn't help but miss the man he had been. Tears began swimming their way around my eyeballs and readied themselves to take the plunge yet again. I couldn't let him see me cry. It confused him too much, made him uncomfortable, uneasy. The few times I had let some slip by he knew something was wrong, that I was sad. Yet, trying to understand was overwhelming for him. He didn't know what to say or do to make it better. I was left with keeping them hidden. It was easier this way.

I crawled in next to him lying atop the covers, his face just inches from mine and I let my eyes close. Maybe I would actually get to rest a bit. But it wasn't to be. I soon felt that stare; the one you know is looking right at you, almost into your soul. It made my eyes pop open.

"I have to tell you something." Graham was restless. Uncomfortable. I was sure we'd be taking a trip to the bathroom.

"You have to promise me something." It was the way he said it. Desperate. Pleading. His eyes searched mine, moving back and forth. They looked so big against his skinny face and prominent cheekbones. I looked at him more closely, trying to understand where he was going.

"Okay." I propped my hand under my head and waited.

"You have to promise that you're going to believe all I tell you." I nodded quickly, unable to say anything. His eyes were the clearest I had seen since the accident. All the lights were on. The fog lifted. I was completely intrigued. And stunned at the same time.

"Something happened to me, something remarkable but I'm afraid to tell you. I'm afraid of what you'll think."

"You can tell me." I was sure he was confused. He'd have questions. He always did. Questions about how he got here, the wreck. Crockett. And why nothing seemed to make sense in his mind. I'd then have to explain everything all over again, going through every detail only to have it all forgotten in less than five minutes. It happened most every day now. Sometimes all day.

I breathed big, ready to re-live that night once again so he could rest easy and get some sleep. My heart broke as I couldn't help but feel the deep gut-wrenching sorrow one gets for a person like this. A person as disoriented and confused as him.

But, there was something different about the way he was talking this time. Something about those eyes that made me stop, my swirling thoughts and story-telling disappearing from my mind completely.

"I had an experience. Something I don't think I can fully understand yet. Like a dream, yet it wasn't. It was reality. It was truth. And I was living it." He paused a moment, not out of confusion or lack of clarity; rather it was fear of what I'd think that made him stop short. But he chose to continue.

"It was from the Lord, I know it." His voice was confident again, clear. Just like the old Graham. He sounded so normal. So natural. There were no slurring sounds like the drunk he usually resembled. No jumbled words. No mixed messages. Hearing him talk this way took my voice. I couldn't speak, my own mind stumbling to figure it out. And like roles switching at the last minute, I was now the one with the lost and bewildered mind.

Tears sprang to his eyes and flowed down his cheeks in a uniform fashion. But this didn't stop him. In fact, he found his voice quickly, sure and without any falter.

"I don't know how I got there, but I found myself in a huge open area, like a parking lot; only bigger. There was nothing to my right. Nothing to my left. But in front of me a lone tree grew. Huge yet inviting, it looked like a willow tree. Except, I somehow knew this was no ordinary willow tree." He sank a breath and continued on.

"I looked down. My feet were on blocks, placed perfectly next to each other, lain out and sunk into the ground. I was on a road of some sort, the placement of these blocks, so strikingly perfect, it made me peer closer. There were no gaps in them. No cracks. No blemish of any kind. They were flat and even with each other, their edges coped down a bit giving them a smoother appearance. It wasn't that sharp look you sometimes see in tiled bathrooms or malls. This was worn yet somehow perfect. They were rectangular, about 8 inches wide and 12 inches long."

"I don't know why their size stuck out to me." He almost laughed, his eyes somewhere else while he re-lived whatever it was he saw.

"Randi?" He was looking at me now, his attention back here with me.

"Yes?" Like I was reading a good book I had been completely sucked in, waiting, unable to turn the pages fast enough.

"Each block, and there were more than I could ever count, were made of solid gold." The hair on my neck began to rise, and I felt my arm hair go too.

He didn't wait for me to play catch up or say something to make him stop. He was all in now.

"I thought I should head to this tree, the one in the middle of all that open space. It was the only thing around."

"Up close it was even bigger than I first thought, its branches hanging low and thick with some so long they touched the golden floor. They brushed the ground back and forth, back and forth like a gentle caress, a soft tickle."

"They continued to sway, some sort of wind or force caused them to move. Their color fascinated me. Light, pure and white, pumped through their very veins. The closest thing I can think to describe them is Christmas lights; but it was obvious no one had ever hung these. These were permanent, grafted in, part of the branch. And it was beautiful. I reached out and touched one. Alive. Real. Amazing."

"While I stood admiring, that small gust of wind came again and moved the branches revealing the trunk and base of the tree. It was open for me to see under and I stood there looking in from the outside.

"People were sitting there. Heads bent. Eyes closed. I had to take a closer look. I had to see what they were doing."

"What were they doing?" I couldn't wait. I had to know.

"They were praying."

"I could hear them too. Some were speaking English. Some were speaking Chinese. But I could still make out their words. Their language. It was the strangest thing—being able to understand them."

I couldn't believe what he was telling me. Many Chinese people had heard of his injuries through friends, missionary friends, their prayers and fasting for a complete stranger had been a humbling experience for me. But, I had yet to share any of this with Graham. He wasn't ready. He wouldn't have understood yet.

So I thought.

His tears picked back up as he fought the emotion racking his heart.

"Every one under that tree was praying for *me*. For *my* healing." A sob escaped his mouth and he gulped to gain control. I was crying too, unable to hide it any longer.

"There's more." He said.

"I could hear music. Lots of music. Each song different from the next, yet playing and flowing together into one big song. There were hundreds playing. Somehow these prayers fit into the song as well. It was unlike anything I had ever heard. The most beautiful of sounds."

"The branches from the tree stilled creating a curtain for me to hide behind with all the others. I couldn't see out, but knew if I wanted to continue to the other side I could."

"I had to keep looking for someone to help me. Someone to tell me what was going on and where I was. All I wanted was to come home to you. I knew I was far away from all I had known, from all that was familiar to me."

"And that's when I saw him. There under the tree, sitting on a stump, a piece sticking out the side of the tree itself like a seat, was my dad. He was busy holding a walking stick with both hands, his head bent with the stick between his legs. The rod worked its way back and forth quickly like he was chiseling something, moving the earth or dirt, which surrounded the base of the tree. He was working so hard at this job he couldn't see me. He didn't know I was standing just over his shoulder."

My mind imagined Gary sitting as Graham described. His hands burning from the work, his head bent low with the task at hand. Somehow I knew the reason why Gary had been there. It had been his prayers, like this stick working and working. Plowing and plowing their way to the throne of Grace. Gary wasn't going to give up, his prayers were the loudest of all, the most determined, the most unwavering for his son.

"My dad finally looked up at me, and I could hear my voice pleading for him to show me the way home. Or to someone who could help me."

"But he wouldn't say a word even as I begged him over and over, my face wet with my tears. He just kept moving that stick back and forth. Back and forth. It was moving so fast. Maybe he couldn't hear me. The work he was doing, the prayers too much for him to focus on me or anyone else. I was beginning to get desperate and about to panic when he took one of his hands off the stick and pointed it beyond the tree's branches. Just outside it, to the other side."

"I looked up, thinking without a doubt there'd be help beyond that tree, the one with all those lighted branches. They swayed one last time, allowing me to walk through easily. Sure enough a figure was there. He stood still. He stood alone. He watched the busyness under the tree like a parent watching their children from a distance."

"He was waiting for me as if he knew I'd come. He *must've* known I was coming. And he was ready. I walked toward him suddenly hit with a feeling of recognition. I knew this guy. And he knew me. Somehow I knew he'd be able to help me. I knew he'd have the answers I sought. And I knew everything was going to be okay. An amazing peace flooded my entire being."

"He stood there, a simple man with a face I had never seen before. But it was soft with kind eyes and blondish hair. I wondered if it was the light making his hair appear the way it did, bright, shiny, almost white."

"There was nothing extraordinary about him. Nothing worth noting. He wasn't big, he wasn't small. Just average. I knew when I looked deeper, staring into His eyes with His own peering back that I was standing in front of Someone great, Someone worth great praise."

"Who?" I couldn't wait to know.

"It was Him. It was Jesus." He whispered this.

My mind and heart were racing as one—ultra fast, thundering almost out of control. I was once again left speechless.

"I couldn't speak. I couldn't find the words to say. They had all been taken. The realization of Who I was standing with hit me like a ton of bricks. I don't know how I didn't fall at His feet."

"He told me to follow Him. That I'd need to keep up. And with that He turned fast leading the way. Without hesitation I followed."

"I had to run to keep up, He was going so fast, the golden road disappearing under foot. We soon found ourselves in a meadow, running through grass, jumping over logs and streams. It started to look more like home, like things I was comfortable with."

"Everything grew darker with a path in front and me barely making it out, but I kept on, knowing in my heart it was the right way to go. I must've lost sight of Jesus completely. I knew He was still here, still with me, but I couldn't make Him out with my eyes anymore. It was growing so dark."

"What happened next?" I asked when he grew quiet and distant.

"The last thing I remember is stepping over a log, my feet tired and weary from running. I opened my eyes and was in a room. There were chairs lined on one side, a small table on the other."

He began describing his room at the rehab hospital. And he was describing it perfectly.

He stopped talking now. His stare penetrating me.

"I know it sounds crazy. I was never one to believe that this kind of stuff actually happened to people. But this couldn't have felt more real. I was there."

His tears had lessoned now, with a few still wetting his face. He wiped some away and sniffed.

I leaned in closer making sure he could see me. My heart.

"I believe you Graham. With my whole being I believe what you're telling me." I gripped his hand, his good one and clung tight. It was what we were going to have to do. Hold on and cling tight. To each other. To God. To His promises. To all He had done and all He was still going to do. It was never clearer to me in this moment that His plan rang supreme. That all this was part of something bigger. Something Graham had a small glimpse of.

I finally arrived at the corral, the wheelchair locking into a perfect spot next to the fence. I whistled for Crockett. But, I hadn't needed to. Crockett knew who was there to see him. With nose stretched out and Graham's right hand extended up, the two touched for the first time since that awful night. Maybe it was the way Crockett sniffed him, or held his nose there much longer than normal. Maybe it was Graham's gentle touch, unchanged and completely familiar, something only he could know.

Crockett's breath had to be warm on Graham's skin blowing just like it had that day in a round pen so long ago when hand and nose met in that first horseman's handshake. It had started as man and beast. Horse and horseman. But on this day, the end of summer within grasp, these two became much more. Their story was just warming up, their bond stronger than ever. Nothing could stop them now, their momentum too fast, too powerful. They'd continue to fight their battles together. Learn together. Ride together. Continue on. *Together*. As friends. As brothers.

I could see The Dark Stretch continuing on for miles yet, and I knew I'd never get off. This was where I belonged now. This was where I fit. And it wasn't all bad. I'd keep racing. I'd keep pressing on. I could do it because I had the best Horseman who ever lived taking me to where the darkness would one day meet the Light.

EPILOGUE

September 29th, 2010

He stood fully dressed in baggy jeans, sneakers and a zip-up jacket. He looked frail, but he was having no more of that chair and the hold it had on him. It had served him well but now sat idle in the corner of the room. Unused and no longer depended upon, the chair seemed almost sad and lonely, like it was missing its partner.

He wouldn't remember this moment. He wouldn't know the importance of this day. But I would. And I took special care to fill my mind's deepest parts with remembering all the misty eyes from the staff, the smiles from the therapists and the joy from everyone else. My own tears were hard to resist as he signed his own release papers. It was a final test for him.

I was too emotional to say much to Fallon or any of them for that matter. I simply gave out hugs, a quiet 'thank you' escaping my shaky lips. I wasn't worried. They knew my heart. They could see how grateful I truly was.

It was a quiet homecoming for Graham, the fall sun cast its shadows long and deep. It was just the kind of day I wanted. Our kids and a few family members were about as much as he could handle. Becoming over stimulated was something I had to be careful about.

It would be some time before he remembered much, his short-term memory damaged and hard for him to understand. In many ways, he was still in a coma, a walking, talking, somehow functioning coma. It would be months for the fog to completely lift off him, for him not to feel this was all just some strange dream he was forced to live.

In all his forgetfulness, miss-matched words and troubled mind, he was adamant on two things: his love for me and that time he spent with the Lord near the willow tree.

He never remembered telling me that first time in our bed, the tears so real and raw. But the experience would end up being one of the only things he could remember. He'd tell it again and again to me, never once changing the story, never once confused. It was the only thing he was sure of during that time of sleep, coma and never ending therapy.

He lost two years of memories, erased like a chalkboard. He'd never remembered that night. He'd never remember riding in the sport he loved. And our youngest son, Keith, was all but forgotten to him.

Still, we had no choice but to continue on. We had to hold tight to the memories we did have and start making new ones right away, even if I'd be the only one to remember them.

He would eventually return to work, left with a limp of sorts and many scars. We like to look at these as reminders of all the Lord has done. Not something to bring us down.

Through it all, Graham remained true to himself and his God. And he has been blessed because of it. An unexpected baby came two years after his accident. A little girl. She remains another part of the miracle, a special piece to the story. She represents the undeniable grace and love the Lord continues to shower onto us. There wasn't any debate as to what we would call her.

We named her Fallon.

ACKNOWLEDGMENTS

My most sincere thanks to my Savior and King. It was Your love, Your faithfulness that carried me through the darkest of hours. You gave me what I needed to move mountains. And just look at how far they've moved.

My deepest thanks to those there that night. To the lady I have yet to thank personally for supporting a fragile neck and head. The first responders, the EMT's, firefighters, pilots, nurses, doctors. Your quick response, your professionalism is to be commended.

It was amazing to watch my community come together. Your love and support for us was overwhelming and humbling.

The staff at The Sunnyview Rehabilitation Hospital will always hold a special place in my heart. Thank you to the nurses, therapists, and aides for all your hard work, dedication and love you showed to my family.

My wrangler family will never be forgotten. I thought I was touching your lives but all along you were touching mine. I was honored to work with you, sweat with you and race against you. "Git yer hats on!"

My church family will perhaps never be the same. I am proud of you, as is the Lord. Thank you to my editor, Jenae Edwards. You came to me at just the right time.

Christine, your guidance, prayer, support and love during this journey of mine has been so influential in my life. Your wisdom has been a blessing to me. Thank you.

A special thanks to my Grandfather, Kenneth Vander Wiele. You've supported me in so many ways; I know you will always be one of my biggest fans. Thank you for believing in me.

It is said in times like this there is nothing like family. It's true. I wasn't the only one put through the fire. I wasn't the only one hurting, sad and waiting for answers. We all were. I am honored to have stood in those hot flames with you! Thank you for *everything*.

My parents remain my biggest heroes and my favorite love story to watch. You have shown me what it's really like to love as Jesus does, serve like Jesus and work hard for what you want. In my writings you must know pieces of you will always be sprinkled throughout each line. I love you.

Not every wife gets the blessing of marrying into such an amazing family as I have. Mom and Dad Stump, you are not my in-laws; you are not Graham's parents. You are my own. My second set. And I love you as such. Thanks for being there, for supporting me, for loving me as only you two can.

Dan and Bonnie thank you for dropping your lives to come take care of mine. You loved my kids and sacrificed your time to love my own. Thank you forever!

Graham, you are my best friend, my secret crush and the coolest guy in any room. Thank you for teaching me what true love is. Thank you for saying yes to me and more importantly to the Lord.

ABOUT THE AUTHOR

Randi Stump was born and raised into the beautiful Adirondack Mountains in upstate New York. She was always most comfortable on the back of a horse and soon realized a career with these animals was her calling. She received a degree in Equine Science and Management from SUNY Morrisville and soon married the love of her life, Graham. She served seven years as Horsemanship Director at the Word of Life Ranch where she instructed and taught children, teens and young adults the art of horsemanship.

Graham and Randi reside together in Schroon Lake, New York with their three children, Wyatt, Keith and Fallon. They lead a simple and quiet life in the woods where they enjoy their horses, dogs and all the mountains have to offer.

Follow more of their story on Randi's blog at www.grahamandrandi.wordpress.com.